STANDARD BANKING

The Solution to America's Monetary Crisis

By David R Young

Volume 3 of the Freedom vs Enslavement Series

ISBN: 978-0-9858707-5-1

Published by DRY Productions

Cover design by D.R. Young

Printed in the United States of America

For information or bulk orders, contact:
DRYoung.Freedom@gmail.com

Also by David R Young

<u>Freedom vs Enslavement Series</u>

Book 1: THE POLITICAL SPECTRUM
Freedom vs Enslavement

Book 2: 110 DAYS OF SLAVE LABOR
How the National Debt Enslaves Your Labor
and the Constitutional Solution to End It.

Dedication

To Thomas Jefferson and Alexander Hamilton whose visions inspired this book

Acknowledgements

I would like to thank Anthropic's Claude AI for its assistance in researching information, compiling data, formatting and editing, and as a sounding board for ideas and concepts. It has been an invaluable tool to handle the mechanics of writing while freeing up my attention to create this work.

I would also like to acknowledge ChatGPT for its ability to review and edit this book as a secondary check, since AI can make mistakes.

I want to acknowledge my wife for putting up with my neglect of household duties and lack of attention to her while I spent all my “free time” creating this work.

Table of Contents

Introduction

FIRE!

This is NOT a drill!

Your grocery bill has jumped 40% in the last decade—and half of that happened in just the last three years. Your paycheck buys less every month.

The dollar has lost 97% of its value since 1913. Banks are no longer required to hold reserves. There is $38 trillion in debt. Growing $1 trillion every 100 days. This predicts an accelerating breakdown in the monetary system within the next decade if not reversed.

Each of these facts will become evident as you understand how money and banking actually work.

The fire is REAL. The timeline is SHORT.

But panic would only make it worse. You still have time to understand what's happening and why. When you act, it must be with knowledge and deliberate intention. You need to be the adult in the room to help bring order to the chaos.

The first thing to know about this is that you can't control what you don't understand. To bring order to the chaos, you need to understand how banking actually works—the simple mechanics behind the system.

Once you see the basics, everything else will become clear.

Let's start...

Chapter One

BANKING

Its Origins and Fundamental Principles From Goldsmiths to Modern Money

The Goldsmith's Discovery

Before we can understand what went wrong with banking—and how to fix it—we need to understand what banking actually is. Not the jargon-filled version from business schools. The fundamental reality that existed before central banks, before the Federal Reserve, before the system became deliberately complicated to hide the corrupt intentions of those who perverted its true purpose.

Banking began with a simple problem and an elegant solution.

Picture yourself as a London merchant in the 1600s. You've accumulated gold coins through successful trade. You have a problem: where do you keep your wealth safe?

Your home isn't secure. Thieves are common. Fires destroy entire neighborhoods. Even the Tower of London, once trusted for storage, had proven unreliable when Charles I seized merchants' gold in

1640 to fund his wars. You need somewhere to store your gold that won't be stolen or lost.

Then you notice something. The goldsmith down the street—the craftsman who makes jewelry and works with precious metals—has something you don't: a massive iron vault. He needs it to protect his raw materials and finished products. His vault is the most secure storage in the neighborhood.

So you approach him with a proposal: "I'll pay you a small fee if you'll store my gold in your vault."

The goldsmith agrees. He counts your gold, records the amount, and gives you a receipt. The receipt states: "This certifies that John Smith has deposited 100 gold coins with Thomas the Goldsmith, redeemable on demand."

You walk away with a piece of paper. The goldsmith has your gold. And here is what makes this arrangement work: You trust that goldsmith.

Security and Trust make the storage system work.

The Birth of Negotiable Receipts

Initially, when you needed gold, you'd return to the goldsmith with your receipt, he'd give you back your coins, and that was that.

But then something interesting happened that would change commerce forever.

You needed to purchase wool in bulk from a farmer to sell in your trade. When you returned to the goldsmith to withdraw some of your gold for this large purchase, the goldsmith offered a simpler solution: he could issue two receipts—one for you (80 coins) and one made out to the farmer (20 coins).

The farmer accepted the 20-coin receipt. A week later, he needed to buy seed from a merchant. Instead of going to the goldsmith to withdraw the gold, he did something simpler: he signed the back of the receipt, transferring it to the merchant. The merchant could now take it to the goldsmith and collect the 20 coins—or sign it over to someone else for his own purchases.

This practice spread quickly. Receipts began circulating from hand to hand, each holder signing them over to the next. The goldsmith's receipts had become a form of money themselves.

This is called a negotiable receipt. It became known in legal and banking terms as a negotiable instrument (a formal document that creates legal obligations). "Negotiable" simply means it can be transferred from one person to another. The receipt represented real gold in the vault, and crucially, the goldsmith remained obligated to honor the receipt regardless of who held it—the legal claim to the gold moved with the paper.

For the modern reader: Think of this like a check. You write a check, it represents money in your bank account, and the recipient can deposit it or potentially endorse it to someone else. The principle is the same. Checks are negotiable instruments—the modern version of those goldsmith receipts.

For bankers: You recognize this as the foundation of commercial paper and the concept of negotiability under the Uniform Commercial Code (UCC). But originally, it was just common sense—paper representing real value that people trusted enough to trade.

The key point: These receipts were backed by actual gold sitting in the goldsmith's vault. The receipt was a claim on real wealth, not wealth itself. But because people trusted the goldsmith, the receipts circulated as if they were gold.

From Goldsmith to Banker

By the mid-1600s, after merchants shifted to storing their gold with goldsmiths rather than the Tower of London, the goldsmiths made an observation. Their vaults stayed full. On any given day, only a fraction of depositors came to withdraw gold. Most were content using the receipts.

Consider a typical goldsmith's situation: He has 1,000 gold coins in his vault, belonging to various depositors. On any given day, perhaps only 100 coins are withdrawn. The other 900 sit idle while the receipts circulate as money.

So he thinks: "I have all this gold sitting here doing nothing. What if I lent some of it out and charged interest?"

The goldsmith offered depositors a proposition: instead of paying a storage fee, they could allow him to lend a portion of their deposits to productive borrowers and earn interest in return. These depositors understood their gold might be out on loan, but they trusted the goldsmith would maintain enough reserves to meet normal withdrawals. In exchange for accepting this arrangement, they not only avoided the storage fee but received a share of the interest the goldsmith earned from his loans. These depositors became, in effect, investors in the goldsmith's lending business.

Not all depositors chose this arrangement. Some preferred security—their gold always available on demand with no lending. Perhaps they didn't yet trust the lending system, or perhaps they needed their funds readily accessible for daily business needs rather than long-term investment. For these depositors, the goldsmith provided pure storage for a fee, keeping their full deposits in the vault at all times. Later, this would be known as 'running cash' or demand deposits.

With investment depositors in place, the goldsmith could now make productive loans. Here's how it worked:

A furniture maker comes to him: "I need to buy better tools and more wood. I'm turning away customers because I can't keep up with demand. If I had 100 gold coins, I could expand my production, take those orders, and earn enough profit to pay you back with interest."

The goldsmith considers this. He has 1,000 coins in the vault. Even if several depositors showed up at once, they'd probably only want 100-200 coins total. He could safely lend 100 coins and still have plenty to meet any withdrawals.

So he makes the loan. The furniture maker gets 100 gold coins, buys tools and materials, produces more furniture, sells it, and pays back the loan with interest.

Everyone benefits:

The furniture maker expanded his business

The goldsmith earned interest

The community now has more furniture

The original depositors' gold remained safe and with added interest their balances expanded

The furniture maker, now more prosperous, deposited his additional earnings with the goldsmith—increasing the vault's reserves and enabling more productive loans

This is banking in its pure form. The goldsmith has become a banker—an intermediary who holds depositors' wealth safely while lending some of the deposited funds to productive borrowers.

Notice what just happened. The goldsmith connected those who had saved wealth (the depositors) with someone who could use it constructively (the furniture maker). He facilitated production by enabling constructive use of saved wealth, benefiting everyone involved in the arrangement, including the community.

This loan process just described is called fractional reserve banking. The banker keeps some deposits in reserve and lends out the rest. Out of every 3 coins deposited, he keeps 1 in the vault and lends 2.

How Much to Keep, How Much to Lend

Here's the key to sound banking.

If the goldsmith keeps too much in the vault, he's wasting an opportunity to serve productive borrowers. If he lends too much, he risks being unable to meet withdrawal requests.

What happens if he lends out 800 coins, keeping only 200 in reserve?

Now he's vulnerable. If depositors come asking for 300 coins, he can't provide them. If word spreads that he can't honor his receipts, panic sets in. Everyone rushes to withdraw their gold at once—a bank run. The goldsmith fails. Depositors lose their wealth. People who borrowed money might be ruined if their loans are called in early.

Through centuries of experience, sound banking practice established a simple rule: out of every 3 coins deposited, keep 1 in the vault, lend 2. This rule emerged from practical experience. Banks that maintained it survived. Banks that ignored it failed.

The Suffolk Bank in Boston (1825-1858) maintained reserves around this level for 33 years. Scottish banks operated this way for over a century. When the Great Depression hit, Canadian banks with strong reserves survived while thousands of American banks failed. History showed this ratio provided crucial protection.

What Makes Money "Good"

Let's step back and ask a fundamental question: What made those goldsmith receipts work as money?

Four essential characteristics had to be present:

First: the receipts were backed by real value—they represented the gold coins in the vault. The receipt took on the value of the gold it represented. No more, no less.

Second: the goldsmith could only create receipts for gold he actually held. No gold, no receipts.

Third: anyone holding a receipt could walk in and get their gold. No receipt, no gold.

Fourth: people trusted that specific goldsmith. His reputation was his most valuable asset. No trust, no deposits.

When all four characteristics exist, you have sound money. Remove any one, and problems begin.

The Two Types of Lending

The goldsmith-turned-banker now faced a critical question: Which borrowers should he lend to? Not everyone seeking a loan would use the funds in the same way, and this distinction would prove crucial to sound banking.

Let me show you why this matters through two borrowers who walked into a bank on the same day.

The first, a carpenter, wanted $10,000 to buy better tools and hire an apprentice. "I'm turning away work," he explained. "With better equipment and help, I can take those jobs, earn more, and pay you back from my profits."

The second, a clerk, wanted $10,000 for a vacation. "I've been stressed," he said. "I need a break. I'll pay you back from my salary over the next few years."

Both want the same amount. Both might be able to repay. But only one loan creates new wealth.

This reveals two fundamentally different types of lending. Bankers call the first type *primary stage lending*. This finances the creation of new wealth—new goods and services. The furniture maker borrows to buy tools and wood, then produces furniture. A farmer borrows to buy seed and equipment, then grows crops. A manufacturer borrows to build a factory, then produces goods. A cloth merchant borrows to purchase wool from farmers, then sells the finished cloth at profit. In each case, the loan directly enables the creation of something valuable. These products are referred to as *commodities* (physical goods that can be bought, sold, and traded). Real wealth increases in the community. The borrower can repay from the profits of what he produced.

The second type is called *secondary stage lending*. A home mortgage finances the purchase of an existing house from one owner to another. A car loan finances the purchase of an existing car from dealer to buyer. Personal loans consolidate existing debt. Credit card debt finances consumption of goods already made. These loans don't create new products or services—they simply move already-created goods from one person to another. They can be useful—people need homes and cars. But they're fundamentally different from primary stage lending.

Here's why this matters: When banks focus mainly on secondary stage lending, they stop serving production. They're just helping people buy and sell things that already exist—and collecting interest every time something changes hands. Without loans for production, fewer new goods get created. New jobs aren't created. When production doesn't expand, people can't earn the money they need to buy commodities. Standards of living begin to decline.

Sound banking prioritizes primary stage lending—financing production. The borrower creates something valuable, sells it, earns profit, repays the loan with interest, and everyone benefits. This reveals a vital purpose of banking: to increase production, which then increases the prosperity of the community it serves.

Money as Commodity Receipts

Here's a useful way to think about money that will help you understand everything that follows: Money can be viewed as a receipt for deposited commodities.

In the goldsmith example, the receipt represented deposited gold in his vault. The gold had value—people wanted it. The receipt represented the value of that gold.

But the principle extends further. When you work, you create something others want and need. The doctor heals patients. The farmer grows wheat. The carpenter builds furniture. These things have value because people want them, like the gold in the goldsmith's vault.

Expand this concept to the whole economy: Society becomes the vault holding all these things everyone produces. When you deposit what you've produced into this vault, you receive money—a receipt proving you contributed something. You can then trade that receipt for what others have deposited. The farmer's receipt (money) can claim the doctor's healing. The doctor's receipt can claim the farmer's wheat. The carpenter's receipt can claim both.

Money facilitates this exchange. It's the receipt system that allows people to efficiently trade what they've created without needing direct barter.

The system depends on everyone who wants to claim value actually producing something of value. A child doesn't produce yet, but his parents share their receipts with him—their production supports his consumption. As the child grows, he begins contributing. He does chores for his family, mows lawns for neighbors, helps at a local shop. He starts depositing his products and services into these smaller economies—his household, his neighborhood—and receives payment for them. He's learning the fundamental principle: to claim value from society's vault, you must deposit value into it.

But what about an adult who chooses not to produce? He has no receipts because he deposited nothing into society's vault. If he still wants to eat, to live in shelter, to consume what others produced, he must either start producing—or take by force what he hasn't earned. Theft becomes his only option. This reveals why sound money matters: when money truly represents production, anyone living honestly must contribute something of value to society. When the criminal ends up in jail, he receives minimal sustenance—shelter and food—but at society's expense. The successful effort to rehabilitate criminals to become contributing members of society not only saves a life from despair, but adds additional production and value to the society.

Then there are those who cannot produce—the severely disabled, the elderly who can no longer work. Traditionally, families cared for their own, and communities supported those without family through churches and voluntary associations. People freely chose to share their receipts with those in need. Volunteering in this way deposits a person's time into society without taking receipts, but provides them for another. There are people able and willing to do this, receiving their exchange through the goodness and well-being that such actions bring. When these methods fail to provide for this non-productive portion of society, it falls on government, which collects taxes—taking receipts by force—to fund welfare programs. This is the least responsible method, removing both the voluntary choice to help and the direct connection between giver and receiver.

This also helps one understand how someone becomes wealthy. He must create an abundance of a wanted commodity and deposit it into society. All successful people don't just produce something—they make it possible for others to produce. A business owner like our furniture manufacturer hires workers so they too can produce. The furniture is his commodity, but he pays them for their production—the actual furniture they create. Their payment depends on what they produce, not simply their time. When this production expands from a single community to a state or nation, the wealth generated for the owner grows very high indeed.

And this is the concept of money and its value, and the fundamentals of prosperity.

The Goldsmith's Limitation

Here's what kept the goldsmith-banker honest: Competition kept him in check. If he charged too much interest or provided poor service, depositors and borrowers would use a different goldsmith. He was a known member of the community—his personal reputation was at stake. He served one town or neighborhood, so his power was geographically constrained. He operated under the same laws as everyone else. If he failed, he personally lost everything. His own wealth backed his operations.

These limitations created a natural check on abuse. The system wasn't perfect. Some goldsmiths committed fraud, some made poor loans and failed. Sound practices were rewarded, fraud was punished, and the competitive marketplace sorted good bankers from bad.

So banking, in its pure form, emerged as a natural solution to the problem of storing and moving value safely. The goldsmith became a banker not through decree or special privilege, but through providing genuine service that made commerce easier and safer for everyone involved.

This is banking at its origin—storing value, issuing receipts, lending to productive borrowers while maintaining reserves. These are its fundamental principles.

Now that you understand these origins and principles—how receipts represent value, how reserves protect depositors, how primary stage lending creates production—three questions remain: What is banking's legitimate purpose? How do we build a system from these fundamentals that cannot fail? And how do we measure whether a banking system serves prosperity or betrays it?

These questions lead us to Standard Banking.

Chapter Two

STANDARD BANKING

The Solution for Economic Stability & Prosperity

Chapter One revealed the fundamentals of banking. In this chapter, we apply those fundamentals to build a system called Standard Banking.

First, we'll identify the goal of banking. Then we will establish the purposes needed to reach that goal. We will also formulate policies that translate these purposes into actions and requirements for good banking.

The objective of this chapter is to familiarize the reader with the activity of banking so they can easily recognize and evaluate the integrity and trustworthiness of any bank.

What is the Goal of Standard Banking?

The goal of any endeavor sets the long-range objective one is striving for. A football team sets a goal to win the Superbowl. Identifying one's goal gives you direction. There is a lot of study, planning and work that goes into reaching any goal. It doesn't just happen.

After reading and understanding Chapter One, you likely could work out the goal of banking. How would you apply those fundamentals and toward what end? It would likely be:

GOAL: To safeguard the wealth of a community and to utilize this stored wealth to increase the production capacity of valuable commodities, which increases the prosperity and survival of the individual, group, or nation it serves.

Another way of looking at this is that banking exists to connect those who have saved value (depositors) with those who can create new value (borrowers), turning stored wealth into productive capacity.

Breaking this down further, what purposes would support this goal?

The Purposes of Standard Banking

Purposes are the shorter range objectives, that combined makes it possible to obtain the overall objective. For the football team, it would be things like drafting high quality players, maintaining player's health, having them in top shape, coordinating their activity to make them into a real team, and to get them on board to reach that goal of winning the Superbowl. These things don't happen on their own.

A team has to be established and they must know what needs to be done, and get it done. And they must be dedicated to the goal and each other to reach that final objective. It is a lot of hard work! But you never hear them complain as they heft that trophy over their heads.

Any broad goal requires identifying the purposes. These purposes cannot just repeat the goal. They must address all aspects of life as they apply to the banker, staff, depositors and borrowers. This is the team. All four.

And it is necessary that all four understand the game. Only then can each take responsibility for their part and hold each other accountable.

PURPOSE 1 (For the banker and his family)

To provide the banker with an honorable livelihood through services that increase community prosperity.

The banker earns income and gains status within the community through his service. His success is aligned with the community's success. This applies to the banking staff as well.

PURPOSE 2 (Serving individual depositors)

To safely preserve depositors' wealth according to their agreement with the bank, providing storage only, or as an investment partnership.

Historical goldsmith banking offered two account types:

Running Cash (Withdraw on Demand): Gold stayed fully reserved, never lent. The depositor paid a storage fee and had immediate availability.

The bank made a profit on storage only.

Investment Deposits: Gold partially lent (one-third in reserve, two-thirds to productive borrowers). The depositor earned interest and accepted risk, becoming an investor in the lending business under the control of the goldsmith.

Both depositors got exactly what they contracted for. Running cash stayed fully reserved. Investment deposits maintained sound ratios (minimum one-third) while the remainder financed production. Complete transparency. No hidden speculation.

In *The Creature from Jekyll Island*, G. Edward Griffin argues that any fractional reserve banking constitutes fraud and that only 100% reserves are honest banking. Griffin's position correctly identifies the problem with corrupt banking, but he failed to identify that some banking institutions managed to maintain fractional banking successfully, as shown in the examples given in this book. Instead, he advocates pure warehousing where banks hold all deposits without lending and charge storage fees. This eliminates banking fraud, but it also eliminates banking and its productive function: turning savings into production that increases community prosperity.

Standard Banking solves this through informed consent and account structure. Accounts for pure storage maintain 100% reserves—exactly what Griffin advocates. Depositors who want pure storage, get pure storage. Investment accounts operate at 33% reserves, but depositors choosing these accounts understand they are investors in the lending business, sharing both risks and rewards. The fraud Griffin correctly condemns occurs when banks apply fractional reserves to all deposits without distinction, without disclosure, without consent. Standard Banking eliminates that fraud through transparency and choice while preserving banking's productive function. The historical examples—Suffolk, Scotland, Canada—prove this works when the correct purposes and policies govern operations.

PURPOSE 3 (Benefits creatively-productive community members and the community as a whole)

To efficiently direct capital to productive borrowers who create valuable commodities for use within and outside the community.

The bank connects savers with producers. It actively directs capital toward borrowers who create new commodities, new services, new prosperity. The bank's judgment directly affects community productive capacity.

PURPOSE 4 (Regarding group stability and trust)

To maintain sound reserves ensuring bank stability and community trust.

Sound reserves (minimum one-third for investment deposits, full reserves for running cash) create stability. Depositors trust their savings are safe. Borrowers trust they can get capital. Currency holds value. This foundation makes everything else possible.

PURPOSE 5 (Trade between communities, states, and nations)

To facilitate trade and exchange of commodities across communities, states, and nations.

Each productive loan---each factory, farm, and business---creates commodities that can be traded beyond the local community. Standard Banking enables this exchange, connecting producers across regions and borders. Trade increases prosperity for all parties. Communities specialize in various technologies, either learned or developed, and the commodities produced are exchanged with others. A higher standard of living only emerges through expanded commerce (production and trade).

One can see this in the reduced living standards in the U.S. since major industry shifted to other countries. Those countries have increased their production, raised their standards of living while our nation favored consuming over producing. The only road toward prosperity is increasing production capacity and increasing valuable commodities, and this is accomplished by standard banking.

PURPOSE 6 (Infrastructure, buildings, and commodities)

To finance improvements to physical infrastructure and environment which assist production and trade.

Standard Banking finances infrastructure. Typically this is done in coordination with government, using community funds for such improvements. The productive borrower builds something real, lasting, and valuable such as roads, bridges, buildings, and irrigation. The physical universe becomes more ordered, and more useful for the communities long term survival.

PURPOSE 7 (The individual spiritually)

To operate with integrity, honoring the sacred trust placed in the profession.

Banking is built entirely on trust. A person hands his wealth to a banker because of trust. The borrower receives capital based on trust.

Receipts (currency) circulate based on trust. Break that trust; lie, cheat, or gamble with depositor funds, issue receipts without backing, and you violate something sacred. You betray the principle that makes civilization possible: the ability to trust your fellow man with something of value.

These are the purposes gleaned from the fundamentals covered in Chapter One. From these we start to build something good, something trustworthy. Now we look at how each person in this economic chain maintains this trust and what happens when it isn't kept.

The Test

When a community demands and maintains Standard Banking, (operating according to these seven purposes), ALL spheres of life benefit with minimum harm. This is the natural result when the system operates according to its true purposes.

What does this look like when a banker puts his own needs above everyone else's, becomes "greedy"? You can test corrupt banking against these same purposes, which influence various aspects of life. Who does corruption benefit?

Corrupt banking benefits the corrupt banker (self), but harms depositors through loss of wealth, traps borrowers through unpayable debt, harms families through economic stress, extracts wealth from the community by inflating the currency, impoverishes the community and surrounding communities, causes unnecessary stress to all including the corrupt banker himself, and violates natural law.

Corrupt banking benefits ONE splinter of life while harming SEVEN others. By this test---greatest good for greatest number---corrupt banking is profoundly, destructively unethical.

What This Means for You

For citizens: You now have a framework for evaluating any banking system. Does it serve all these purposes? Does it benefit you across multiple spheres, or extract from you to benefit others?

For bankers: You have a mirror. Look at these purposes against what you actually do. Are you fulfilling them? Or have you been forced---by regulation, by the system, by the structure you inherited---to violate them?

Most bankers entered the profession with good intentions. You wanted to serve your community, do honest work, help people prosper, and of course, prosper yourself. These seven purposes may resonate with what you thought you'd be doing.

But intentions don't matter if the system is designed to violate these purposes. The question isn't whether individual bankers are good or bad. The question is whether the current banking system you work within actually fulfills these purposes or violates them.

That question can only be answered by measuring the system against its own stated goals and comparing those goals to the purposes of Standard Banking.

The Nine Fundamental Policies

To achieve these seven purposes, Standard Banking would operate according to nine fundamental policies. These are essential. Violate them, and you are no longer practicing Standard Banking.

POLICY 1: All receipts backed by real commodities

All receipts issued must be backed by real commodities---either deposited (as in running cash accounts with 100% reserves) or consigned through productive loans that create new commodities. Money represents real value, not promises.

POLICY 2: Reserves maintained at sound ratios

Banks shall maintain distinct account types with appropriate reserve requirements:

100% Reserve Accounts (Running Cash/Demand Deposits): Full reserves always maintained. Deposits never lent out. Available on demand. Depositor pays storage fee. Pure storage contract.

Higher Reserve Tier (50% Reserve): Moderate reserves for conservative investors. No storage fee. Available with notice or modest restrictions. More conservative risk profile.

Standard Investment Tier (33% Reserve): Minimum one-third reserves (3:1 maximum lending ratio). Free storage PLUS interest share. Depositor is investor in lending business. Shares in interest profits. Accepts lending risk.

All depositors must be clearly informed of distinctions and choose which account type suits their needs. Contract clarity and depositor choice are mandatory.

POLICY **3: Primary stage productive lending priority**

Capital shall be allocated primarily to productive borrowers creating new commodities. Finance creation of new exchangeable commodities, not transfer of existing wealth. Ninety-five percent of lending should create something that didn't exist before.

POLICY 4: All lending within depositor risk tolerance

All lending must be within depositor risk tolerance. Depositors must be clearly informed of which account tier they've selected and what that tier means.

The bank discloses the reserve ratio maintained for their tier and the availability terms---whether funds are available on demand or with notice. The bank explains the cost or compensation structure---whether the depositor pays a storage fee or receives interest share.

Most importantly, depositors understand the risks they accept through their tier choice. Depositors choosing investment tiers (50% or 33% reserve) explicitly accept lending risk in exchange for interest share.

No deposit may be lent without the depositor's informed consent through account tier selection.

POLICY 5: Complete transparency in operations

Full disclosure to depositors of reserve ratios, lending activities, and bank financial condition through regular statistical reports.

Transparency isn't optional---it's foundational.

POLICY 6: Personal liability maintained

Bankers remain personally responsible for losses resulting from violations of Standard Banking principles. When you have skin in the game, you're careful.

POLICY 7: No special legal privileges

No government bailouts, no special protections. Operate under contract law like any other business. Accept no government protection, bailouts, or immunity from consequences of unsound practices.

POLICY 8: Community General Liability Fund (optional)

Separate fund for natural disasters affecting the entire community, funded through voluntary community assessments, held securely but separate from bank operations, used exclusively for rebuilding destroyed productive capacity after natural disasters.

POLICY 9: Absolute integrity in reporting and oversight

All statistical reports reflecting the truth. Independent oversight regularly examining reporting for accuracy. Severe penalties for any intentional false reporting including full personal liability and permanent removal from banking.

False reporting betrays the trust on which everything depends. Integrity is non-negotiable.

Historical Proof: Standard Banking in Action

What you're about to see are real banking systems that operated according to these principles. As you read these examples, notice which purposes and policies appear in action. You'll see real reserves backing obligations, personal liability keeping bankers honest, market discipline sorting sound banks from unsound ones, transparency allowing depositors to verify claims, and competition rewarding service over exploitation.

The Suffolk Bank System (1825-1858)

Picture Boston in 1825. Banks across New England issued their own paper notes---sounds chaotic, right? Enter the Suffolk Bank. Some clever bankers realized that if they collected notes from all the country banks and showed up regularly demanding physical assets, bad banks would fold quickly and good banks would stay honest. By 1838, over 300 banks participated. The system ran for 33 years with banknotes maintaining their face value throughout the entire region. Bank failure rates for member banks: 6.8% compared to non-members at 14.5%. No taxpayer bailouts, no "too big to fail" justifications, no Federal Reserve printing trillions.

Just bankers keeping other bankers honest because their reputation depended on it. The system ended in 1858 not because it failed, but because a competitor bank used state legislation to push Suffolk out of the note-collection business. The competitor failed to maintain the same discipline, and the New England banking system became less stable---proving the system worked when the principles were followed.

Scottish Free Banking (1716-1845)

Scotland ran competitive banking for 129 years with no central bank, no monopoly on currency issue, no government telling banks what to do. Just banks competing for customers by being sound, reliable, and trustworthy.

The result? Scotland's bank failure rate was 0.4%. England, with its mighty Bank of England and government privileges? 1.81% failure rate---more than four times higher. Scottish notes were accepted at full value everywhere because everyone knew they were good. When one bank's notes showed up at another bank's counter, they got exchanged for gold fast. This kept everyone honest without a single government regulator.

Scotland's economy went from roughly half of England's GDP per capita in the mid-1700s to nearly equal by the mid-1800s. Standard Banking actually helps people build wealth. The system ended in 1845 not because it failed, but because the British government imposed new banking regulations requiring government charters and restrictions---central banking was becoming fashionable, and governments wanted more control over money.

What Made It Work

Workable banking is based on actions that are constructive and beneficial to the banker, his clients, and his community. It has been that way since the goldsmiths and will continue that way into the future. The purposes and policies distilled from hundreds of years of successful banking provide stable principles that are unchanging.

These principles were available throughout history. Sound banking systems operated successfully for centuries. The evidence was there. The question was whether anyone would take responsibility for implementing them consistently.

Now YOU understand these principles. YOU can recognize sound banking from corrupt banking.

YOU can evaluate any system against these purposes and policies. The question is whether YOU will act on this knowledge to bring sound banking into existence.

What Comes Next

But first, we need to confront what stands in the way. We will evaluate the Federal Reserve system---which every bank in America operates under---against both its own promises and the principles of Standard Banking just established.

The Fed was created in 1913 with specific purposes: maximum employment, stable prices, moderate interest rates, and financial system stability.

After more than a century of operation, we can measure results against these promises.

Let's see if the Fed serves constructively or destructively, fulfills Standard Banking or violates it, increases prosperity or extracts it.

Chapter Three

MEASURING THE FEDERAL RESERVE

We've established the seven purposes of Standard Banking---the principles that turn savings into production. Now let's examine the institution that controls American banking: the Federal Reserve.

We're not going to dive into the Federal Reserve's origins or the political maneuvering that created it in 1913. If you want that history, see *110 Days of Slave Labor* (Volume 2 of the Freedom vs Enslavement series) which covers the Fed's creation in detail, along with other excellent books listed in the references at the back of this book.

What we're interested in now are the facts as they exist today---facts anyone can verify by looking at the Fed's own statements and the measurable results of its policies.

So here's what we'll do: take the Federal Reserve's own stated objectives and measure them against 110 years of actual results. You can judge for yourself what the facts reveal.

The Fed's Stated Goals

According to the Federal Reserve's own website, its main objectives are:

1. 1. Maximum Employment - Keep unemployment low
2. 2. Stable Prices - Control inflation, maintain purchasing power of the dollar
3. 3. Moderate Long-term Interest Rates - Keep borrowing costs reasonable
4. 4. Financial System Stability - Prevent banking crises and panics

These sound like reasonable and valuable objectives, don't they? A central bank managing the money supply efficiently to ensure jobs, stable prices, reasonable rates, and no more financial panics.

Did you notice anything missing from what you learned in Chapter Two? These objectives focus on managing economic activity---employment levels, price stability, interest rates, crisis prevention. Absent is any mention of what actually creates prosperity: increasing production, financing productive enterprise, turning savings into wealth. It seems the Fed aims to manage the economy without addressing what makes an economy productive.

Let's measure how they have done over the past 100 plus years.

SECTION 1: Maximum Employment

Goal: Keep unemployment low and stable.

The Record:

Since the Fed's creation in 1913, we've experienced the Great Depression with 25% unemployment, multiple recessions with unemployment spikes, the 2008 crisis hitting 10% unemployment, and repeated boom-bust cycles that destroy jobs.

But here's what most people don't understand about how these cycles actually occur.

How the Fed Creates Boom-Bust Cycles

Imagine you're a business owner---let's say you manufacture furniture. You employ twenty people. Business is steady. You're making decent profit, planning moderate expansion.

Then the Federal Reserve decides the economy needs "stimulation." They lower interest rates dramatically. Suddenly, borrowing money becomes very cheap. Your banker calls you up: "Hey, we can give you a loan at 3% interest. You've been wanting to expand, right?"

You think about it. At 3%, you could borrow $500,000, buy new equipment, hire ten more workers, and increase production. The numbers work and you take the loan.

But you're not the only one. Every business owner in America is getting the same call. Cheap money is suddenly available everywhere. So everyone expands at once.

The Boom Phase:

Now there's a hiring frenzy. You need ten workers, but so does every other manufacturer in your area. Wages start rising because everyone's competing for the same pool of workers. You hire your ten people. Your competitors hire theirs. Unemployment drops, and politicians praise the Fed for "creating jobs."

With all these artificially low rates available, your customers have easy credit too. They're buying more furniture. Business is booming. You're running at full capacity. Life is good.

All across the economy, this same pattern repeats. Construction companies building like crazy. Manufacturers expanding. Retail stores opening new locations. Everyone hiring. The economy looks fantastic.

What You Don't See Coming:

So here's the problem---and it's a problem the Fed created, not you.

All this expansion isn't based on real sustainable demand. It's based on artificially cheap credit. You expanded because money was cheap, not because of organic consumer demand. Your competitors expanded for the same reason. Everyone expanded simultaneously because the Fed made money cheap for everyone at once.

Now there's massive overcapacity in your industry. You can produce twice as much furniture, but consumers don't actually need twice as much furniture. Your competitors are in the same boat. There are too many furniture manufacturers chasing the same customers.

And you and everyone else who took these loans are now further in debt.

The Contraction Phase:

Then the Fed looks at all this "overheating" (the overheating they created by making money too cheap) and decides they need to "cool things down." They start raising interest rates. Fast.

Your loan that was at 3%? New borrowing is now at 7%. Then 9%. Then 12%.

Suddenly the numbers don't work anymore. That expansion you did at 3% interest made sense. Now at 12% interest? You're losing money on those loans. You can't refinance---rates are too high. You can't borrow more to cover the difference, it's too expensive.

Your customers are hit the same way. They were buying furniture on easy credit. Now credit cards are at 18%, home equity loans are expensive, and they stop buying. Demand drops.

You're running that expanded facility with forty-five employees, but you have half the orders coming in. Your company is bleeding money.

What do you do? You lay people off. Cut back to thirty employees. Then twenty-five. If it gets bad enough, back to your original twenty---or fewer.

But you're not the only one. Every business that expanded during the boom is now contracting during the bust. Mass layoffs happen simultaneously, just like mass hiring happened simultaneously.

The Fed's Role

The Fed created both phases, contrary to its stated purposes.

The boom wasn't natural market growth---it was artificially stimulated by the Fed's low interest rates. The bust wasn't a natural correction---it was the inevitable result of that artificial stimulus being withdrawn.

If interest rates had stayed stable and reasonable the whole time, production would have expanded slowly, based on real demand, at a sustainable pace. Some businesses would grow, others would shrink, but there wouldn't be this violent boom-bust cycle affecting everyone at once.

Instead, the Fed's artificially low rates made expansion look profitable when it wasn't sustainable. Businesses made rational decisions based on those rates. Then the Fed raised rates, turning sound business decisions into disasters. They engineered both the boom and the bust---then called the bust a "crisis" that requires their intervention, more artificially low rates, which starts the whole cycle over again.

Why would they do this?

Follow the money. The boom-bust cycle is profitable for those who control it. Banks and connected insiders profit during booms, acquire assets cheap during busts, and receive taxpayer bailouts when they fail.

Here's a real example of how it works: Timothy Geithner served as President of the New York Federal Reserve Bank during the 2008 financial crisis. In that role, he helped decide which banks would receive taxpayer-funded bailouts and how much they'd get. Major banks—JPMorgan Chase, Goldman Sachs, Citigroup—received billions in rescue money that Geithner approved.

When Geithner left government service in 2013, where did he go? He went to work for Warburg Pincus, a private investment firm closely connected to the same Wall Street banks he'd just rescued. Warburg Pincus works with these major banks, invests their money, and maintains deep financial relationships with them. Geithner personally received over $2 million per year in salary—a massive increase from his government pay.

Think about that: While at the Fed, Geithner used taxpayer money to rescue Wall Street banks. Then those same banks' financial partners hired him and paid him millions. He wasn't rewarded for serving taxpayers. He was rewarded for serving the banks.

This isn't unique. It's the pattern: Fed officials create policies that rescue major banks with taxpayer money. Then those same banks—or firms closely connected to them—hire the Fed officials who rescued them, paying them millions. The revolving door between the Federal Reserve and Wall Street ensures that Fed policy serves the banks that will later employ Fed officials. (For a comprehensive timeline of the Fed-Wall Street revolving door showing who went where and what they earned, see Appendix Y.)

But it's not just Fed officials who profit from the boom-bust cycle. The banks themselves profit most when businesses fail.

In Standard Banking, the bank's success is tied to the borrower's success. If your business fails, the bank loses too—which keeps bankers careful about who they lend to and incentivizes them to help productive enterprises succeed. The bank wants you to thrive because your prosperity is their prosperity.

But under the Fed system, major banks discovered they could profit more from business failures than from business success. Let me show you how this worked in 2008 with a real example.

Construction companies across America expanded during the housing boom. Take a mid-size residential construction firm in Arizona—similar companies existed in every state. In 2004, when the Fed had rates at 1%, the company borrowed $2 million at 4% interest to buy equipment, hire crews, and build spec homes. The math worked. Housing prices were rising 15-20% annually. Business was booming.

The bank collected healthy interest payments for three years. Profit number one.

Then the Fed raised rates seventeen times between 2004 and 2006, pushing from 1% to 5.25%. The construction company's credit lines—tied to prime rate—went from 4% to 9%. Their monthly interest payments more than doubled. Meanwhile, home buyers faced the same rate shock. Mortgages became expensive. Demand collapsed.

The construction company had equipment, half-built homes, and loans they could no longer service. They tried to refinance. Banks said no—rates were too high, and the housing market was tanking. In 2008, the company declared bankruptcy.

Here's where it gets interesting.

The bank foreclosed on everything. The construction equipment—excavators, trucks, tools worth $500,000 new—sold at bankruptcy auction for $85,000. The bank bought it through a subsidiary. The half-completed homes, purchased for land value, maybe 30 cents on the dollar. The bank acquired valuable assets for a fraction of their worth. That's profit number two.

But the bank still showed a "loss" on the loan because the $2 million loan was only partially recovered through foreclosure. So the bank reported it as a bad loan, part of their mortgage crisis losses. And then—profit number three—the bank received taxpayer bailout money through TARP (Troubled Asset Relief Program) to cover those "losses."

Let's count: The bank collected three years of interest payments (profit one), acquired valuable assets at bankruptcy prices (profit two), and received taxpayer money to cover the "loss" (profit three).

The construction company owner lost his business, his equipment, his employees, and his savings. Many of these owners lost their homes too, having personally guaranteed the loans. Some declared personal bankruptcy. Some never recovered.

The bank reported record profits within two years.

Under Standard Banking, this couldn't happen. No bailouts exist. No Fed manipulation creates artificial booms and busts. Banks maintain real reserves and can't make reckless loans because they're personally liable for losses. If a bank makes a bad loan and the business fails, the bank loses money—real money, from their reserves and shareholders. This creates the right incentive: help borrowers succeed, because their failure is your failure too. The bank becomes your partner in production, not your predator waiting for the Fed-created crisis.

The Pattern Since 1913

This has happened repeatedly since the Fed's creation. In the 1920s, easy money fueled a stock market boom and massive expansion, then the Fed contracted in 1929, triggering the Great Depression and mass unemployment. The 1990s brought easy money and the dot-com boom with everyone hiring, followed by Fed contraction in 2001, the dot-com bust, and layoffs. The 2000s saw easy money create a housing boom with construction everywhere, then the Fed contracted in 2008, causing a housing bust and millions unemployed. The 2010s brought more easy money to "rescue" the economy, inflating everything, and the 2020s added even more easy money during COVID, followed by Fed rate increases---continuing the same destructive pattern.

So does monetary manipulation create jobs, or just shift them around while creating instability?

Real jobs come from productive enterprises creating goods and services people want. Printing money doesn't create productive capacity---it just inflates prices (by creating more money than there are valuable commodities, reducing the value of each dollar) and encourages speculation, which depresses production.

The Fed doesn't stabilize employment. The Fed destabilizes it---then exploits each crisis to seize more power. The 2008 crisis led to Fed authority over non-banks and mortgage markets. The 2020 crisis led to unlimited money creation and corporate bond purchases. These are just two examples from a century-long pattern: each disaster the Fed engineers becomes justification for removing another constraint on its authority. Instead of enforcing Standard Banking principles, the Fed uses each new power to create the next crisis through artificially low rates and speculation, perpetuating the cycle. (For a complete timeline of Fed power expansion through manufactured crises, see Appendix X.)

For detailed employment statistics comparing the Fed era to pre-Fed banking, visit the Bureau of Labor Statistics historical database at bls.gov or search "BLS historical unemployment rates."

SECTION 2: Stable Prices

Goal: Control inflation and maintain the dollar's purchasing power.

The Record:

It takes about thirty dollars today to buy what one dollar bought in 1913.

That's a 97% loss of value in the dollar measured against goods and services.

But measured against what the dollar actually was—a receipt for gold—the loss is even worse.

To make this real: In 1913, your dollar was backed by gold—1/20th of an ounce, to be exact (twenty dollars equaled one ounce of gold). That same amount of gold today is worth about $211. If you'd held your wealth as that gold dollar instead of converting to paper dollars, that 1913 dollar would have 211 times the purchasing power it has today. The dollar was a receipt for real value. Today it's a promise backed by nothing.

How did we get from gold-backed dollars to worthless paper? The Fed orchestrated it step by step.

When the Fed was created in 1913, your dollar was still redeemable for gold. But the Fed immediately began printing more dollars than gold existed to back them. By the 1920s, they had created far more paper receipts than gold in the vault—the classic goldsmith fraud from Chapter One, but executed by a central bank with government protection.

In 1933, the Fed convinced President Roosevelt to confiscate private gold ownership. Suddenly, citizens couldn't redeem their dollars for gold anymore. The gold stayed in government vaults while the Fed kept printing dollars. You held receipts; they held your gold.

In 1944, the Bretton Woods agreement limited gold redemption to foreign governments only. American citizens were completely cut off from the gold their dollars supposedly represented.

By 1971, foreign governments started demanding their gold. President Nixon gets blamed for "closing the gold window" that year, ending all gold convertibility. But Nixon didn't create this crisis—the Fed did. Nixon simply admitted what the Fed's printing press had already made inevitable: the receipts no longer represented real gold.

The Fed systematically destroyed the gold standard over 58 years, then let a president take the blame for the final step.

But they weren't done. In 2020, the Fed's Board of Governors took the final step in removing all constraints on money creation. They eliminated reserve requirements entirely. Zero reserves required. The Fed can now create unlimited dollars, and banks can lend unlimited amounts, all backed by nothing, constrained by nothing, answerable to no one.

The result of this systematic destruction of sound money shows up in everyday prices. In 1913, a pound of coffee cost fifteen cents. Today, that same pound costs about $14. Your great-grandfather's fifteen cents had real purchasing power. Your fourteen dollars buys what his fifteen cents did—but you need over ninety times as much coin to buy it.

Let that sink in. Under the Federal Reserve's stewardship---under their explicit mandate to maintain "stable prices"---the dollar has lost essentially all its value over 111 years.

Question: If your goal is price stability and you achieve a 97% loss, have you succeeded or failed?

For purchasing power comparisons and inflation calculations, visit the Bureau of Labor Statistics CPI Inflation Calculator at bls.gov/data/inflation_calculator.htm.

SECTION 3: Moderate Long-term Interest Rates

Goal: Keep borrowing costs reasonable and stable.

The Fed claims to maintain "moderate" long-term interest rates. Let's see what that looks like in practice.

During COVID, borrowing rates started around 5%, dropped to 3.25%, then shot back over 8% within two years. After the 2008 crisis, rates fell from 8% to near 2% and stayed low for seven years before climbing back. The most extreme swing came in the early 1980s: borrowing rates spiked from 12% to over 21% by 1981, then plummeted back down over the next few years.

Do these wild swings constitute "moderate" rates?

When rates are artificially low, bad investments that should never happen suddenly look attractive. When rates spike, good businesses that were viable at normal rates suddenly fail. The rate manipulation prevents efficient capital allocation and destroys productive enterprises that can't adapt to rapid changes.

The Fed's rate manipulation has failed to produce moderate, stable borrowing costs. In fact, their policies are counter to their stated purposes. They create the same boom-bust cycles we saw destroying employment in Section 1—wild swings that benefit those who control the cycle while devastating productive businesses.

SECTION 4: Prevent Financial Crises

Goal: One of the Fed's primary founding justifications was to PREVENT banking panics and financial crises. The 1907 panic was used as "proof" that America needed a central bank.

The Promise: "With expert management, scientific monetary policy, and a lender of last resort, we can prevent the boom-bust cycles."

The Fed's Record Since 1913

Major financial crises occurred AFTER the Fed was created to prevent them: the 1920-21 Depression; the Great Depression (1929-1939)---the worst economic catastrophe in American history just 16 years after the Fed's creation; the 1970s Stagflation with simultaneously high inflation and high unemployment that economists said was impossible; the 1987 Stock Market Crash losing 22% in one day; the S&L Crisis (1980s-90s) with over 1,000 institutions failed; the Dot-Com Crash (2000-2002) where internet companies with no profits were valued at billions for having ".com" in their names, Fed's artificially low rates fueled wild speculation, then when rates rose hundreds of companies went bankrupt and trillions in "wealth" evaporated; the 2008 Financial Crisis requiring trillions in bailouts through TARP (Troubled Asset Relief Program); and the 2020 COVID Crisis where the Fed printed over $4 trillion in a matter of months with predictable severe inflation as money supply exploded while goods and services didn't.

The Free Banking Era Comparison

The "Free Banking Era" (1837-1862) is often cited as proof that banking without central control leads to chaos. But what was it actually? During this period, individual banks issued their own currency—paper notes backed by their reserves—and competed for customers based on the soundness of their money. No central bank existed to control money supply or rescue failed banks. Market discipline was the only regulator. (For a detailed history of the Free Banking Era, see *110 Days of Slave Labor*, Volume 2 of the Freedom vs Enslavement Series.)

Compare the actual results.

During Free Banking, crises recovered relatively quickly. The Panic of 1857 took 1-2 years to recover. The Panic of 1873 took roughly 5-6 years. The Great Depression under the Fed took over 10 years and required a world war to be fully resolved.

Why did Free Banking crises resolve in 1-6 years while the Great Depression dragged on for over a decade? The answer reveals the Fed's violation of Standard Banking principles: focusing on credit manipulation instead of financing the production needed to rebuild lost wealth.

During Free Banking crises, failed businesses closed quickly. Prices fell, making goods affordable again. Private producers rebuilt without government interference, and production resumed. And as covered earlier, production creates wealth.

The Great Depression lasted because the Fed and government doubled down on this mistake. The Fed first contracted money supply (causing the crash), then expanded it without effect. New Deal programs focused on government employment and redistribution rather than unleashing private productive capacity. Some policies actively reduced production—paying farmers not to produce, for example. The constant regulatory uncertainty discouraged private investment.

Only World War II ended the Depression—not because of monetary policy, but because government finally demanded massive private production. Factories building ships, planes, and weapons at scale. Private productive capacity unleashed. That's what Standard Banking does: it finances production, which creates real wealth. The Fed finances speculation and government spending, which doesn't.

The Fed also created a new problem entirely absent from Free Banking: taxpayer-funded bailouts. When Free Banking banks failed, depositors and shareholders lost money, but taxpayers paid nothing. In 2008 and 2020, taxpayers funded trillions in rescues while bank executives kept their jobs and bonuses—a pattern impossible under Free Banking's market discipline.

To be clear: This is not a bid to return to the Free Banking Era. It had its problems---bank failures, fraud, speculative bubbles, painful losses for depositors. It wasn't a workable system either.

But what's remarkable is this random, somewhat wild period of American banking---with no central control, no "expert management," no scientific monetary policy---still produced better results by nearly every measurable standard than the centrally controlled Federal Reserve system we've had for over a hundred years.

That should tell you our current central banking system neither operates on sound principles nor works.

The worst part is, you probably didn't even know. And, you may not have, until now, understood how utterly bad this is.

SECTION 5: Sound Banking? Not Even Close

So that's the Fed measured against its own four stated goals. Complete failure on all counts.

But what about Standard Banking's seven purposes? The Fed sets the policies that govern how all American banks must operate. Let's measure these policies against Standard Banking principles from Chapter 2.

Does the Fed's regulatory framework enable banks to fulfill the seven purposes that actually serve all spheres of existence and benefit everyone? Here's what we find:

Purpose 1 - Provide the banker with an honorable livelihood through service? The Fed's policies create a system where bankers profit most from crisis and instability. When boom-bust cycles hit, major banks receive bailouts and executives keep bonuses while community banks fail. The Fed's framework rewards financial manipulation over genuine service. So if by "service" you mean "extracting wealth from working Americans," then yes, the system works perfectly for that.

Purpose 2 - Safely preserve depositors' wealth? The Fed's systematic inflation policy destroys the purchasing power of depositors' stored wealth. Wealth that depositors saved through productive labor gets steadily confiscated. The Fed's policies make it impossible for banks to preserve depositor wealth---the currency itself loses value by design.

Purpose 3 - Direct capital toward productive borrowers? The Fed's policies actively incentivize secondary stage lending over primary stage production financing. Cheap money policies make speculation more profitable than production. While some productive lending still happens, Fed policies channel capital toward financial manipulation, corporate stock buybacks, and asset bubbles rather than genuine wealth creation. The framework systematically misdirects capital away from producers toward speculators.

Purpose 4 - Maintain sound reserves? The Fed eliminated reserve requirements entirely. Banks can now lend every dollar deposited with nothing held back. The Fed's policy creates a system where dollars have nothing backing them. Standard Banking requires 33% reserves. The Fed requires zero.

Purpose 5 - Increases production capacity of the community, state or nation? The Fed's policies expand money supply far faster than production capacity expands. This is backwards. Standard Banking finances production, which naturally limits money supply growth to match real wealth creation. The Fed prints money without requiring corresponding production, actively undermining this purpose.

Purpose 6 - Finance infrastructure improvements? The Fed's policies enable government deficit spending without requiring productive investment. Infrastructure decays while money gets printed for consumption rather than construction. The 2025 American Society of Civil Engineers gave U.S. infrastructure an overall C grade---"not in good state of repair." The Fed's framework allows infrastructure neglect while financing grows elsewhere.

Purpose 7 - Operate with integrity? The Fed operates with no real oversight. Attempts to audit the Fed have failed for decades. The Fed claims such accountability would "compromise political independence"---meaning they refuse transparency. Standard Banking requires complete honesty in all reporting. The Fed's policies institutionalize opacity, making genuine integrity structurally impossible.

Scorecard: 0 out of 7 purposes fulfilled. 7 out of 7 violated.

The Federal Reserve's policies make Standard Banking impossible. Every principle that would enable sound banking---reserves, productive lending priority, wealth preservation, infrastructure investment, transparency, integrity---the Fed's framework systematically undermines or prohibits.

Now, the last point on this subject is the subject of how a group or organization demonstrates insanity.

As George Orwell said in 1949

> *"The Ministry of Peace concerns itself with war, the Ministry of Truth with lies, the Ministry of Love with torture, and the Ministry of Plenty with starvation."*

And here we have the Federal Reserve which concerns itself with debt and zero reserves.

It has been said that insanity is that point where the person or group steps over into being more destructive than constructive.

By all accounts we are dealing with an insane group that calls itself The Federal Reserve. And it's been said many times, "it's not Federal" and now can be added, "it has no reserves".

Its actions are destructive to the economy and to the welfare of those their own purposes are supposed to help. Help is not help when it destroys. That is true insanity.

Even they know their castles are burning. How do we know this?

Chapter Four

FEDERAL RESERVE SYSTEM CRISIS

This chapter explains why a Standard Banking system needs to be started now, not eventually.

The current monetary system is collapsing. Those who created the problem are already planning their "solution"---one that preserves their ill gotten power while restructuring the system on their terms.

There will be a reset. The question is: Will it be theirs or one that we create?

They Know It's Coming

Remember how Chapter 3 ended? "Even they know their castles are burning. How do we know?"

They've told us so.

Not in plain language to the general public, of course. But in the careful, technical language they use with each other, the warnings are clear.

The Bank for International Settlements---the umbrella organization of the world's central banks, essentially the central bank of central banks---recently warned that rising government debt is creating "heightened risks for the stability of the global financial system." They project sovereign debt will reach 120% of GDP in advanced economies by 2030. Translation: The debt is growing so large it threatens to bring down the entire banking system.

The International Monetary Fund (IMF) warned that "if improvements in governments' primary balance cannot be achieved to offset higher real rates and lower potential growth, sovereign debt will continue to grow," testing the health of the financial sector. Translation: If governments can't dramatically cut spending or raise taxes (and they can't politically), the debt will keep growing until something breaks. IMF head Kristalina Georgieva said her worries about collapse of private credit markets "sometimes keep her awake at night."

The Governor of the Bank of England warned that the situation has "worrying echoes of the 2008 financial crisis."

These aren't conspiracy theorists or doomsday bloggers. These are the people running the system.

They know what's coming. And they have a plan for what comes after.

The Great Reset---Their Solution

In June 2020, the World Economic Forum (WEF) officially launched something called "The Great Reset Initiative."

It's official policy, openly promoted by Klaus Schwab (founder of the World Economic Forum), Kristalina Georgieva (head of the IMF), and various world leaders.

The stated objective? To support economic recovery from COVID-19 and create a "new equilibrium among political, economic, social and environmental systems."

Klaus Schwab put it this way: "The pandemic represents a rare but narrow window of opportunity to reflect, reimagine, and reset our world."

The WEF describes this as "a unique opportunity to transform the world and make it a better place."

Notice the language: Crisis as **opportunity**. Collapse as **chance for transformation**.

They're not trying to prevent the collapse. They're preparing to manage it and use it to restructure the system.

What does that restructuring look like? They call it "stakeholder capitalism"---a system where a self-selected group of "stakeholders" (major corporations, NGOs [Non-Government Organizations], international organizations, and government officials) make decisions on behalf of people, replacing what they call outdated democratic models with "multi-stakeholder partnerships."

Read that again: **Replacing democratic models** with partnerships between unelected global elites, major corporations, and compliant governments.

This is their solution to the crisis they created. Not accountability. Not Standard Banking. Not local control or individual freedom. **More centralized power** in the hands of those who caused the problem.

They're framing the coming collapse not as the failure of their system, but as an opportunity to "build back better" under their guidance. They'll position themselves as the saviors---the experts with the plan to rescue the world from chaos.

And if people are desperate enough, scared enough, hungry enough---they'll accept whatever solution is offered.

Two Paths Forward

Path One: We Wait

Some may want to wait and see what happens. Perhaps the system will somehow stabilize or reform itself. Perhaps debt will stop growing, crises will stop intensifying, the Fed will change its failed policies. Perhaps doing nothing will work out fine.

Then the collapse hits.

When that happens, there is chaos. Panic. Desperation. People who were comfortable yesterday are now scared about feeding their families next week.

Into that chaos steps the "solution"; pre-planned, professionally packaged, backed by all the "experts" and global institutions.

The Great Reset.

"We know you're scared. We have a plan. Trust us. We'll fix this. You just need to accept these new arrangements.

Temporary, of course. For the emergency."

Except the "temporary" measures never end. They never do.

Digital currency they control. Social credit systems. "Public-private partnerships" that are really corporate-government fusion. International institutions with power over local communities. Debt forgiveness that comes with strings---you'll own nothing, and they promise you'll be happy.

And by the time people realize what they've accepted, it's too late.

You can't build an alternative system while living under a fully implemented control structure. The window has closed.

That's Path One. Wait, then accept their reset by default because there's no other option ready.

Path Two: We Build Now

We don't wait for their collapse. We don't wait for their solution. We build Standard Banking at federal and state levels now, before the crisis.

These solutions are detailed in later chapters.

If we act now, we prevent collapse. But even if collapse comes before implementation is complete, at least we know the solution: finish implementing Standard Banking and rebuild our country's economy on **production**, not **debt**.

The Great Reset loses its inevitability because people have choices---and can see which systems actually serve them. We retain local control. We retain freedom. We retain the ability to own property, control our labor, and build wealth.

The Real Choice

After over 100 years of failure, after violating every principle of Standard Banking, after creating a system guaranteed to collapse, replacing our federal economic system is obviously necessary.

When a building is structurally unsound, you don't patch the cracks and hope for the best. You tear it down and build properly. The current system is collapsing. We must replace it with a sound structure built on Constitutional authority and Standard Banking principles.

Not a reset on their terms, but on ours.

Chapter Five

A DECLARATION OF ECONOMIC INDEPENDENCE

In 1776, Thomas Jefferson penned the Declaration of Independence, making clear that to remain subjects of the British Crown meant surrendering control of our lives to distant powers that extracted from us rather than served us. Free people must govern themselves.

Jefferson later warned of another tyranny---one that would arise not through military force, but through control of money:

> *"I believe that banking institutions are more dangerous to our liberties than standing armies. If the American people ever allow private banks to control the issue of their currency, first by inflation, then by deflation, the banks and corporations that will grow up around them will deprive the people of all property until their children wake up homeless on the continent their Fathers conquered."*

The Federal Reserve System is the tyranny Jefferson warned against---private banks masquerading as a government institution, controlling our currency, extracting our wealth through inflation and debt, impoverishing the very people they claim to serve.

We are the children Jefferson described---not yet homeless, but impoverished through monetary manipulation, trapped in unpayable debt, robbed of prosperity our labor should have secured.

Jefferson gave us the Declaration of Independence. This Declaration of Economic Independence expands his work to address the economic tyranny that now threatens the freedom our Founders fought to secure.

THE DECLARATION

When free people find themselves under a banking system that confiscates their labor through inflation, binds their children to debt servitude, and operates through lies and manipulation, they must dissolve these economic bonds and declare the necessities that compel them to independence.

We hold these truths to be self-evident:

That all men are created equal in their right to the fruits of their labor;

That they are endowed by their Creator with certain unalienable Rights, that among these are the ownership of their productive capacity, the preservation of their stored wealth, the protection of their property, and the liberty to trade the value they create;

That to secure these rights, Banking Systems are instituted among Men, deriving their just powers from the voluntary consent of depositors and borrowers;

That whenever any System of Banking becomes destructive of these ends, it is the Right of the People to alter or abolish it, and to establish new Banking, built on principles and organized in ways that will best secure their Economic Safety and Prosperity.

It is recognized that established banking systems shouldn't be changed lightly, and people naturally prefer familiar problems to uncertain change. But when a system faces inevitable collapse, and a long train of abuses reveals deliberate design to reduce people to permanent economic dependence, it becomes their right and their duty to throw off such Banking and provide new guards for their future economic security.

Such has been the patient suffering of the citizens of these States; and such is now the necessity which forces us to replace this System of Central Banking.

The history of the present Federal Reserve System is a history of repeated injuries and usurpations, all structured in a way that establish economic tyranny over the lives of free people.

To prove this, let Facts be submitted to an impartial world:

THE GRIEVANCES

It has hidden its operations from scrutiny, refusing honest accounting while demanding power over every economic transaction.

It operates without accountability to citizens, providing no means to challenge or appeal decisions that destroy their wealth.

It operates outside government control, claiming independence to make monetary policy decisions without approval from the President or Congress, while its actions affect every citizen's economic life.

It has abolished reserves entirely, reducing their required reserves from 18% to zero.

It has created money without backing, issuing receipts for wealth that does not exist.

Through zero reserve requirements and cheap money, it has made financing consumption more attractive than financing production, reducing the nation's capacity to create wealth.

It has made savings lose value by creating inflation that outpaces any interest earned.

It has trapped our government in unpayable debt, requiring endless new borrowing to pay interest on old debt.

It has destroyed the value of our money, reducing the purchasing power of the dollar by ninety-seven percent, confiscating through inflation the stored labor of every citizen.

It has caused repeated economic crises, creating booms through cheap money and busts through expensive money.

It has used trillions in taxpayer money to bail out banks that caused economic crises through unsound practices.

It has created perpetual debt, designing a system wherein the interest owed can never be repaid.

It has purchased government debt with newly created money, enabling unlimited deficit spending.

It has created a system facing inevitable collapse, placing unbearable stress on citizens, businesses, and the banking system itself, while offering no plan for the crisis it has engineered.

The system's deliberate complexity obscures these facts from citizens who don't examine it closely, while those who understand and speak out are dismissed as conspiracy theorists or extremists, their warnings unheeded and their evidence unexamined.

It exists without Constitutional foundation, the Constitution having granted Congress alone the power to coin money and regulate its value, with no provision for private control of the currency.

It was created through deliberate deception, private bankers claiming to establish a public institution while actually creating a system structured in a way that serve their own interests and profit.

These Facts reveal a system built on dishonest and unsound principles, now collapsing. We must therefore act to replace this destructive system and establish Standard Banking that preserves wealth and finances production.

THE DECLARATION OF INTENT

We, therefore, as free citizens of these United States, with integrity of purpose, exercising the Constitutional powers reserved to the States and to the people, do hereby declare:

We declare our economic independence from corrupt banking practices that extract wealth and unconstitutional arrangements that place monetary control outside proper government authority.

We declare a thorough examination of our personal responsibilities, confronting how we enabled this crisis through our silence, our acceptance of convenient lies, and our failure to act when action was required---exercising the self-discipline required to get honest and straight with ourselves.

We declare a complete reorganization of the Federal Reserve system, transforming it from a privately-controlled entity serving banking interests into a Constitutional government agency serving the people, operating under proven principles that preserve wealth and finance production---ensuring this dangerous situation does not repeat.

We declare the establishment of firm policies that will detect and prevent this crisis from recurring---policies requiring proper reserves, transparent operations, personal accountability, and Constitutional limits on government and banking power alike.

We invite every sovereign nation to claim the same independence---sovereignty over their monetary systems, operating under Standard Banking practices that serve rather than enslave.

And for the support of this Declaration, we pledge our voices, our votes, our action, and our determination to make these declarations reality.

This chapter declares the dangerous condition we find our nation in. The next chapters detail how we fulfill these commitments---how we examine our personal responsibilities, reorganize the system to prevent a repeat of this situation, and establish the policies that will detect and prevent the condition from recurring.

This next chapter marks a transition. What follows requires more than understanding; it requires personal responsibility regarding the existing system. The ideas ahead are not complex, but they do ask the reader to confront their role within that system.

Chapter Six

BUILDING YOUR POWER TO ACT

In this chapter, a transgression means acting in ways that conflict with one's stated values, then avoiding that conflict rather than confronting it.

This is not an accusation. It is an invitation to examine one's own participation honestly.

Chapter Five made four declarations. It declared economic independence from corrupt banking. It declared the intention to examine your personal responsibilities. It declared a complete reorganization of the Federal Reserve system. And it declared the establishment of firm policies to prevent recurrence.

This chapter addresses the second declaration: examining your personal responsibilities.

It is a known fact that transgressions reduce one's responsibility in the sphere of the transgression. This is why we have confessions. Depositors, bankers, and politicians have stepped into an existing monetary system. Even if one disagreed with the system, there may not have been much option but to transgress, at least against common sense, and more to the point, against Standard Banking methods.

Why does getting honest about what you've done come before reorganizing the system? Because you cannot build soundly while carrying forward the considerations that allowed corruption to flourish. The Federal Reserve is still there after more than a century. It still exists because we allowed it. We ignored the warning signs, accepted convenient lies and remained silent when we should have done something about it.

Before reorganization can succeed, that silence must end. The lies must be confronted. Personal responsibility must be acknowledged.

This isn't about guilt or shame. This is about getting clean. You cannot build a sound banking system or participate in building one while still under the burden of transgression acquired under the corrupt system.

For Citizens and Depositors

Perhaps you've known something was wrong. Prices kept rising while your paycheck couldn't keep up.

Maybe you deposited your savings without asking what banks did with your money. You might have trusted blindly because the banks looked solid and FDIC insurance made you feel secure.

You know what Standard Banking is now. Use this as your guide in finding what you may have done to transgress against these banking basics.

For Bankers

Perhaps regulations required practices that conflicted with Standard Banking principles. Maybe quarterly pressures demanded growth over stability. You might have made loans, maintained reserves, or focused on certain products because the system required or rewarded it.

You know what Standard Banking is now. Use this as your guide in finding what you may have done to transgress against these banking basics.

For Politicians

You swore an oath to uphold the Constitution. Article I, Section 8 grants Congress, not the Federal Reserve, power over money.

Perhaps you voted for policies that inflated currency, supported bailouts, or approved spending that exceeded revenue. Maybe the system pressured you in ways that conflicted with Constitutional principles or Standard Banking basics.

You know what Standard Banking is now, and what the Constitution requires. Use this as your guide in finding what you may have done to transgress against these basics.

The Process of Getting Honest

This process is personal. It is about your past transgressions and freeing up your future ability to apply Standard Banking. Don't underestimate the need to do this. Done correctly, it can bring great relief.

When you spot a transgression, look it over. When did it happen? What was the type of transgression? (theft, dishonesty, etc.) Where were you when you did it? Review the entire activity from beginning to end. If you find yourself justifying the action, you should recognize these as justifications. (These made it "okay" to do the transgression).

Do this for each transgression you spot.

Why This Comes Before Reorganization

Unexamined considerations that enabled corruption will compromise the new system as they did the old. Without getting honest about what happened previously, the same patterns can repeat.

This examination creates the clarity and increased responsibility required to operate under this new system. Using self-discipline to get honest and straight will give you the power to move forward.

How do we reorganize this corrupt system? What structure prevents these violations from repeating? The next chapter provides the answer.

Chapter Seven

THE FEDERAL BANKING OFFICE

Chapter Five declared economic independence and the intention to reorganize the Federal Reserve system. Chapter Six prepared you by examining your personal responsibilities and building your power to act. The next two chapters establish the structure.

Standard Banking principles mean nothing if the institutions administering them can be corrupted, captured, or circumvented. Replacing corrupt people with honest ones won't work—honest people within corrupt structures become corrupt or ineffective. The structure itself must be replaced. Sound structures make corruption difficult rather than inevitable, enforce Constitutional principles rather than ignore them, and ensure accountability cannot be evaded.

Consider: Every Federal Reserve Chairman has claimed to serve the public interest. Most believed it. Yet each presided over wealth confiscation through inflation, each enabled government deficit spending, each created boom-bust cycles that destroyed families and businesses.

Regardless of intention, the structure produced the same outcome every time.

Consider: Every Congress swears to uphold the Constitution. Most members mean it. Yet Congress routinely violates enumerated powers, spends beyond revenue, delegates authority to unaccountable agencies, and expands federal control beyond anything the Founders envisioned. Their oaths may be sincere, but the structure makes them meaningless.

Consider: Federal agencies claim to protect consumers, ensure safety, and promote welfare. Many employees work diligently. Yet agencies grow beyond Constitutional authority, create regulations with force of law despite lacking legislative power, serve special interests rather than public good, and resist accountability. The employees are often competent and well-meaning. The structure corrupts their work.

You cannot fix a corrupt system by electing or appointing better people to run it. The structure that corrupts them must be reorganized.

This chapter details the Federal Banking Office---the institution that enforces Constitutional fiscal discipline on government spending and Standard Banking principles on the national financial system. Chapter Eight introduces the Office of Constitutional Compliance (the oversight that holds the FBO and all government agencies accountable to Constitutional limits).

Together, these two institutions make the past century's mistakes structurally impossible to repeat.

THE TRIPLE CATASTROPHE OF 1913

Three changes in 1913 fundamentally altered American government, each seemingly small, each catastrophic in consequence, all working together to create the crisis we face now.

The Federal Reserve Act

The Federal Reserve Act of 1913 deceptively established private control over the nation's money supply while disguising it as a government institution. The Act created a system claiming independence from government control while presenting itself as a government institution---a Constitutional contradiction.

This independence placed monetary policy beyond the reach of elected officials. Congress could not oversee policy decisions. The President could not control operations. The American people whose wealth the Fed controlled had no mechanism for accountability. An unelected board made decisions affecting every citizen's economic life without answering to anyone.

The consequences unfolded over decades: unlimited money creation became policy. Inflation became a deliberate tool rather than a failure to prevent. Boom-bust cycles emerged by design rather than accident. Bailouts protected those who caused crises rather than allowing market discipline to correct them. The system now faces inevitable collapse with no plan for the disaster it engineered.

The Sixteenth Amendment

The Sixteenth Amendment (authorizing federal income tax on individuals) fundamentally violated the Founders' design of indirect taxation. The Constitution originally limited federal revenue to tariffs, excise taxes (taxes on specific goods like alcohol or tobacco), and user fees (fees for using government services like patents or national parks). You paid tax when you chose to buy something. You could avoid them.

This aligned government incentives with production. When government revenue comes from taxes on goods, government prospers when production increases. More goods produced means more revenue collected. Government that hinders production cuts its own funding.

The income tax broke this alignment. Now you're taxed simply for working and earning a living—even on retirement income when you're no longer producing. Government can raise rates whether production increases or decreases. Government revenue becomes disconnected from national productivity.

This creates a powerful incentive for government to implement Standard Banking. Sound banking increases production. Increased production means more goods taxed. More goods taxed means more government revenue. The two systems work together—both prosper when the nation produces.

The income tax removed all fiscal discipline from federal operations. When government needed more money, it simply taxed more. No need to justify spending. No need to prioritize among competing demands. No need to live within collected means. The federal government could grow without limit because it could tax without limit.

The Seventeenth Amendment

The Seventeenth Amendment (making Senators elected by popular vote) destroyed the state check on federal power that the Founders carefully designed. The original Constitution established the Senate as representatives of sovereign states, appointed by state legislatures to protect state interests against federal encroachment. Senators answered to state governments, not to popular majorities.

Direct election transformed Senators into national politicians responsive to the same popular pressures driving the House of Representatives. The careful balance between federal and state sovereignty (independent state authority) collapsed. States lost their voice in federal decisions affecting state sovereignty. Two houses of Congress now responded to majority opinion rather than Constitutional structure, accelerating the transformation from republic to democracy.

The Combined Effect

These three changes worked together over 111 years to create the crisis we face now. Federal government grew without limit because nothing stopped it—no budget constraints, no state oversight, no monetary discipline. The dollar lost ninety-seven percent of its value through deliberate inflation. Government debt grew perpetually because government could borrow without limit while the Federal Reserve created money to buy that debt. Banking corruption flourished without accountability, bailouts became routine, and fraud proceeded without prosecution. The republic transformed toward democracy as state representation was replaced by popular vote.

Now we turn from problem to solution: the Federal Banking Office.

THE FEDERAL BANKING OFFICE (FBO)

Constitutional Foundation

The Constitution gives Congress power over money. Article I, Section 8 says Congress has power "to coin Money, regulate the Value thereof." This is legislative power, not executive. Congress makes the rules.

> *"The issuing power of money should be taken from banks and restored to Congress and the people to whom it belongs."*
>
> —Thomas Jefferson

The Federal Reserve violated this Constitutional structure. It claimed independence from government while pretending to be part of government. Monetary authority belongs to Congress, not to an independent agency making policy without Congressional approval.

The FBO restores Constitutional order. Here's how it works: Congress creates the Federal Banking Office through legislation. Congress oversees it. The FBO executes fixed standards set by law—it doesn't make discretionary policy. In this case, Congress decides monetary policy by adopting Standard Banking. The FBO simply executes these standards without deviation. This is Congress exercising its Constitutional authority over money, not delegating that authority to others.

The Federal Reserve Redefined

The term "Federal Reserve" is restored to its plain meaning: the actual commodity reserves held by the federal government backing the currency. Federal Reserve Notes are notes redeemable from these reserves---gold, silver, oil, agricultural products, industrial metals, and government resources.

The Federal Banking Office manages the Federal Reserve by ensuring reserves exist in sufficient quantity to back every dollar in circulation, authorizing new currency only when reserves increase, and gradually reducing money supply that exceeds reserves.

It publishes reserve statistics weekly. Both expansion and contraction occur gradually without shock to the system. This transforms the Federal Reserve from a private institution claiming independence into what it should have been: the people's reserves securing the people's money under Constitutional authority.

In 1974, the United States made an agreement requiring oil purchases worldwide to be conducted in US dollars. This created artificial global demand for dollars, enabling unlimited money printing without immediate inflation at home. That system is now faltering as major oil producers accept other currencies and nations reduce their reliance on the dollar. Standard Banking replaces this artificial demand with actual commodity backing. As the petrodollar agreement ends, commodity reserves become essential for maintaining any international dollar role---not through forced participation but through voluntary choice based on transparent value.

The Critical Innovation

The Federal Banking Office serves as the government's bank. The FBO literally holds all federal revenue, reviews all spending requests against Constitutional and Standard Banking standards, and releases funds only when standards are met. Government operates as a customer of the

FBO, subject to the same principles of Standard Banking we demand from private institutions.

When Congress appropriates funds, the FBO asks the same questions any sound bank would ask: Is this within deposited funds or does it require deficit spending? Does this create productive value or merely transfer wealth? Are emergency reserves (government savings for unexpected crises) maintained at twenty percent? Is this fiscally sustainable or does it create obligations beyond capacity to meet? Is this transparent with public disclosure and measurable results?

If the answers demonstrate fiscal responsibility, funds are released. If the answers reveal Constitutional violations or unsound practices, the appropriation is denied and Congress must revise or override.

This transforms fiscal discipline from political will (which ebbs and flows with electoral pressures) to structural requirement enforced automatically through banking standards.

Leadership: The Federal Banking Officer

One person---the Federal Banking Officer---is responsible for executing the standards Congress adopts for banking and Constitutional limits for government spending.

The Federal Banking Officer is appointed through state legislature confirmation requiring two-thirds approval (more than a simple majority), preventing single-party control and restoring state authority over federal operations. Strict qualifications ensure Constitutional expertise, Standard Banking knowledge, and political independence. The officer serves a six-year renewable term with tiered removal procedures and protection against false accusations. Complete appointment procedures are detailed in Appendix A.

The position carries authority matched by accountability. The FBO operates under annual Congressional authorization that can be withheld if performance fails to meet standards. Quarterly reports to Congressional Banking Committees provide regular oversight of FBO operations and decisions. The Constitutional Compliance Office monitors all FBO actions for Constitutional alignment, with findings published publicly. Personal liability attaches to the FBO for any violations of Standard Banking principles or false reporting, ensuring that consequences for misconduct match the authority exercised.

Division One: Government Fiscal Oversight

All federal revenue flows to the Federal Banking Office and is allocated into three categories: monetary reserves backing the currency, government operating funds available for Constitutional spending, and government emergency reserves (government savings for unexpected crises) building toward twenty percent of annual spending.

The FBO enforces Constitutional limits on new spending. Existing programs like Social Security, Medicare, and Medicaid require separate reform beyond this reorganization's scope. For now, this reform protects beneficiaries by preventing total system failure. Once fiscal stability is achieved, those programs can be addressed through separate legislative processes.

Complete fiscal oversight procedures are detailed in Appendix B.

Division Two: Banking System Regulation

The Federal Banking Office enforces the banking standards Congress establishes. The Standard Banking framework detailed in Chapter 2 sets the benchmark: thirty-three percent reserves, ninety-five percent productive lending, verified reserves, surprise examinations with published results, and no bailouts.

Banks falling below thirty-two percent reserves receive internal notice and must file explanation within forty-eight hours. Banks get ninety days under supervision to restore compliance before public notification. This prevents false accusations while ensuring genuine problems receive attention. Banks unable to restore compliance face public intervention and potential liquidation.

Banks meeting standards operate freely. Banks violating standards face charter revocation. No exceptions, no waivers, no bailouts. Market discipline rewards sound banking and punishes unsound practices through natural consequences.

Complete banking regulation procedures are detailed in Appendix C.

Oversight and Accountability of FBO

Four layers of oversight prevent FBO tyranny:

1. An Inspector General embedded in operations monitoring all decisions and reporting findings to four different authorities: agency head, President, Congress, and Constitutional Guardian

2. Constitutional Review by the Constitutional Compliance Office examining whether FBO actions align with Constitutional principles

3. The Constitutional Guardian tracking patterns and issuing annual public evaluation of FBO performance

4. Complete public transparency with all decisions, IG findings, and Guardian assessments published immediately

This provides multiple accountability paths if the FBO violates Constitutional principles. One layer might fail, but all four failing simultaneously becomes improbable.

Chapter Eight details the Office of Constitutional Compliance providing oversight of the FBO and all government agencies. Complete oversight procedures are detailed in Appendix D.

CONSOLIDATING EXISTING AGENCIES

Creating the FBO requires absorbing, eliminating, or redefining existing agencies to eliminate duplication and streamline oversight.

The Federal Reserve System's twelve Regional Reserve Banks become Regional Divisions of the FBO, serving as field examination offices for their territories. Regional Directors are appointed by the

FBO, serve fixed terms, and rotate among regions to prevent becoming too close to the banks they regulate. The Board of Governors and Federal Open Market Committee are eliminated. The Office of Comptroller of Currency merges into FBO.

The Consumer Financial Protection Bureau is eliminated as Standard Banking principles ensure consumer protection through market discipline.

The Government Accountability Office, Congressional Budget Office, Office of Management and Budget, and Treasury Department continue their current functions. The Federal Deposit Insurance Corporation is reformed to protect depositors without rewarding failed banks—coverage limited to $50,000 per depositor with direct payment to depositors who move funds to compliant banks.

These consolidations eliminate duplicate regulations, conflicting missions, rewarding risky behavior, regulators becoming too close to banks, and waste while streamlining operations and making corruption more difficult.

TRANSITION AND IMPLEMENTATION

The Federal Reserve Reform and Fiscal Responsibility Act creates the FBO through normal legislative process requiring simple majority passage. No Constitutional Amendment needed.

The twelve Regional Reserve Banks are currently private corporations owned by member bank shareholders. Congress created these banks through the Act of 1913. Congress can revoke what Congress created. When Congress revokes the charter, the banks cease to exist as legal entities.

The Reform Act revokes the Federal Reserve Act of 1913, terminating all charters granted under that Act. This is not property seizure—it's withdrawal of a governmental privilege that should never have been granted to private parties. Shareholders own the physical assets (buildings, equipment, infrastructure) that Regional Banks acquired over 111 years.

The Act provides compensation equal to audited book value of these physical assets, paid over five years from FBO operational revenues. Shareholders receive fair value for buildings and equipment but not for lost future profits. Government assumes control immediately. Regional Bank facilities, staff, and systems transfer to FBO on Day One. Operations continue without disruption.

Complete transition procedures are detailed in Appendix E.

CONCLUSION

The Federal Banking Office accomplishes what the Federal Reserve never could: enforce Constitutional fiscal discipline while channeling capital to productive enterprise through Standard Banking principles.

When ninety-five percent of bank lending finances production rather than consumption, the economy creates real wealth. Production increases. National capacity expands. Revenue grows naturally from economic activity rather than taxation. The system funds itself through prosperity, not austerity. Standard Banking directs capital toward productive value, unleashing capacity that benefits everyone through growing wealth.

The result is economic freedom. Currency holds value. Savings accumulate. Opportunity multiplies. Wages rise through genuine demand, not inflation. Citizens keep more of what they earn and direct their own resources. Freedom emerges as natural consequence—capital flows to production, value is preserved, and government operates within fiscal reality.

Most critically, this reorganization prevents another Federal Reserve from emerging. The

Federal Reserve operated for 111 years confiscating wealth, enabling unlimited government growth, and answering to no one. It happened because no safeguards existed to detect and prevent unconstitutional power accumulation. This reorganization makes repetition structurally impossible. Fiscal discipline is enforced before spending occurs. Banking soundness is required through measurable standards. Market discipline operates through natural consequences. Corruption becomes difficult, Constitutional violations expensive, and fiscal irresponsibility transparent.

But power without oversight becomes tyranny. Chapter Eight details the Constitutional Compliance Office---the firm policy that detects deviation before it becomes entrenched, prevents bad banking before it becomes systemic, and secures the liberties of the people. Together, these two institutions ensure the past century's mistakes cannot be repeated.

The window for reform is narrow. The need for action is urgent. The time to act is now.

Chapter Eight

THE OFFICE OF CONSTITUTIONAL COMPLIANCE

Chapter Seven detailed the Federal Banking Office, the institution that enforces Constitutional fiscal discipline on government spending and sound banking principles on the financial system. But power without oversight becomes tyranny. This chapter details the institution that ensures the FBO itself, along with all government agencies, operates according to the Founders' original Constitutional design.

> *"If men were angels, no government would be necessary. If angels were to govern men, neither external nor internal controls on government would be necessary. In framing a government which is to be administered by men over men, the great difficulty lies in this: you must first enable the government to control the governed; and in the next place oblige it to control itself."*
>
> —James Madison

The Office of Constitutional Compliance fills a critical gap that has existed in American government since the founding: no office speaks for the Founders' Constitutional principles before government acts. More importantly, no office systematically asks whether agencies operating today have any Constitutional authority to exist at all.

THE MISSING CHECK

The Founders designed checks and balances to prevent concentration of power. Congress checks the Executive. The Executive checks Congress. Courts check both. States check Federal government. But this system has degraded over the past century. The Seventeenth Amendment removed state representation in the Senate. Federal power expanded far beyond enumerated limits (the specific powers the Constitution grants to federal government). Courts review constitutionality only after implementation, after damage occurs, after taxpayer money is wasted.

A critical gap exists: no institution asks before government acts whether the Founders would have authorized this action. No office systematically examines whether agencies have Constitutional authority to exist. No mechanism makes violations politically expensive before they become entrenched practice.

Consider what currently happens. An agency proposes a new regulation affecting millions of citizens. The regulation goes through internal review, public comment, and implementation. Only years later, after court challenges work through the system, does anyone ask whether the Constitution authorizes this. By then, the agency has staff, budget, constituency groups defending it, and political momentum making reversal nearly impossible.

The Office of Constitutional Compliance fills this gap through two essential functions. First, it systematically reviews every federal agency and program to determine whether Constitutional authority exists for its operation. Second, for agencies that do have Constitutional authority, it ensures they operate within Constitutional limits. This creates prevention before implementation, transparency that makes violations politically expensive, and accountability impossible to evade.

MISSION AND AUTHORITY

The Office operates with a clear two-part mission. The primary mission is determining what belongs in federal government at all—examining every agency and program against enumerated powers in the Constitution, publishing findings on whether Constitutional authority exists, and recommending elimination or transfer to state jurisdiction (state authority and control) for agencies operating beyond federal authority. The secondary mission is ensuring agencies with legitimate Constitutional authority operate in compliance with Constitutional principles—federalism (balance between federal and state power), individual rights, due process, and limited government.

The primary mission represents a fundamental shift: the Office questions whether an agency should exist at all, not just how it operates. If Constitutional authority doesn't exist, the agency shouldn't exist regardless of how well it performs.

The Constitutional basis for this Office is straightforward: Congress has clear authority under Article I to create offices ensuring faithful execution of Constitutional principles. The Constitution itself is the supreme law, and Congress can establish mechanisms to ensure government remains within Constitutional bounds.

The Office cannot override elected officials. Congress retains legislative authority, the President retains executive authority, Courts retain judicial authority. But the Office can publicly identify violations and Constitutional overreach, making it politically expensive to ignore the Founders' design.

When the Office publishes findings that an agency lacks Constitutional authority or that a Constitutional agency is violating principles, citizens can demand action, Congress can investigate, and elections can turn on Constitutional compliance. The Office speaks truth to power but cannot become power itself.

LEADERSHIP: THE CONSTITUTIONAL GUARDIAN

One person holds the office of Constitutional Guardian, appointed through a process ensuring independence from political pressures while maintaining accountability to Constitutional principles. The appointment process itself matters enormously---the wrong process produces a political appointee serving whoever appointed them rather than an independent guardian serving Constitutional principles.

Three appointment options exist: state legislature confirmation (maximum independence, restores state check on federal power), multi-branch panel requiring consensus from Congress, President, and Supreme Court (broad accountability but complicated), or Congressional appointment through super-majority vote (simplest but least independent). The recommendation is state legislature confirmation---requiring a majority of state legislatures to confirm the Constitutional Guardian. This produces someone who can earn trust across diverse state interests and remains accountable to state sovereignty concerns rather than federal political interests, restoring the state voice in federal operations that the Founders designed.

The Constitutional Guardian serves a twelve-year non-renewable term, removable only by two-thirds Congressional vote for Constitutional violations. The long term ensures independence from election cycles. The non-renewable aspect prevents political positioning for reappointment. The difficult removal standard protects against political retaliation while maintaining accountability for actual Constitutional violations.

Qualifications require demonstrated Constitutional scholarship, commitment to originalist interpretation (understanding the Constitution as the Founders intended it, not as modern politics might prefer), no partisan political appointments in the previous fifteen years, and no financial ties to regulated industries. These qualifications ensure the Guardian serves

Constitutional principles, not political parties or special interests.

Complete appointment procedures are detailed in Appendix F.

Division One:
Constitutional Authority and Compliance Review

Division One operates as the investigative and analytical heart of the Office, examining whether agencies should exist at all and whether legitimate agencies operate properly. This division's work breaks into four distinct functions, ordered by priority.

The primary function is Constitutional Authority Inventory---the systematic examination of every federal agency and program to determine whether enumerated powers authorize its existence. This has never been done comprehensively in American history. Agencies were created over decades, each justified at the time, but never reviewed systematically against the Constitutional foundation.

The inventory process works methodically. Division One catalogs every federal agency and program currently operating. For each entity, Constitutional scholars examine Article I Section 8 to determine whether the Constitution authorizes it. The examination produces a clear finding: Constitutional authority exists, or it doesn't.

For entities where Constitutional authority exists, Division One documents which enumerated power provides the basis. For entities where no Constitutional authority exists, Division One recommends either elimination if the function isn't necessary, or transfer to state jurisdiction under the Tenth Amendment if the function serves legitimate purposes beyond federal enumeration.

All findings are published immediately for public scrutiny. Citizens can see which agencies operate with Constitutional authority and which don't. Congress can act on recommendations. States can prepare to receive transferred functions. Agencies cannot hide behind complexity or political protection when their Constitutional foundation is examined publicly.

The target is clear and measurable: one hundred percent of federal government operating within Constitutional authority. Every agency and program either has enumerated power supporting it, or it gets eliminated or transferred. This will shrink federal government substantially while expanding state and local capacity for functions people actually need.

The second function is Constitutional Compliance Review for agencies that have legitimate Constitutional authority. Having authority to exist doesn't mean operating without limits. An agency authorized by Constitutional power must still respect the balance between federal and state authority, protect individual rights, follow laws passed by Congress without creating its own laws through regulation, maintain due process, and operate transparently.

Division One conducts proactive reviews before agencies implement major regulations or programs. The review examines whether proposed action stays within Constitutional limits. Does it respect state jurisdiction? Does it protect individual rights? Is it following the specific powers Congress gave them instead of making up new powers through regulations? The review produces public Constitutional guidance that carries no legal force but makes proceeding after Constitutional warning politically expensive through media coverage, public pressure, and Congressional oversight.

A reasonable concern arises: won't Constitutional review slow government down? This reflects real experience with bureaucratic bottlenecks where everything must be inspected before it can move forward.

The answer lies in what's being reviewed. Constitutional review asks one simple question: does the Constitution authorize this? This differs from inspecting quality or evaluating policy details. Technology could help speed this up—artificial intelligence trained on the Constitution and Founders' writings could provide instant preliminary analysis that scholars verify within days. Minor regulatory actions could get reviewed within 72 hours. Major new programs would take longer, as they should. Getting it right matters more than getting it done fast.

Division One also provides special oversight of the FBO itself. The Federal Banking Office wields enormous power over government spending and the financial system. Regular Constitutional audits ensure the FBO remains within delegated authority, applies spending denials based on legitimate Constitutional principles rather than political bias, and maintains enforcement consistency. The FBO, like every agency, must prove it operates within Constitutional bounds.

The third function is Legislative Review. When major legislation is introduced, Division One examines whether the Constitution authorizes it and publishes the analysis for everyone to see. This gives Congress and citizens Constitutional perspective before voting. The Office cannot stop legislation—only Congress votes on laws—but publishing Constitutional concerns makes it politically harder to pass clearly unconstitutional legislation.

The fourth function is Investigation of alleged Constitutional violations. When violations are reported or discovered, Division One investigates with subpoena power (authority to require testimony and documents), examines evidence, and publishes findings. If criminal violations are found, cases are referred for prosecution. If Constitutional violations are found without criminal element, findings are published for Congressional action and public accountability.

Complete Constitutional Review procedures are detailed in Appendix G.

Division Two:
Inspectors General Consolidation

Every major federal agency currently has an Inspector General (an independent investigator who finds waste, fraud, and abuse). This structure creates a fundamental conflict: IGs report to the agency heads they investigate. This enables pressure, control, and retaliation. An IG who discovers serious problems faces pressure from the agency head who controls their budget, workspace, and career prospects. The incentive is to soften findings, delay reports, or avoid investigating certain areas entirely.

Division Two solves this through complete separation. All IGs are consolidated under Constitutional Compliance Office authority, working physically and administratively separate from the agencies they investigate. Each IG remains assigned to specific agencies but now works from Constitutional Compliance facilities, draws salary from the Constitutional Compliance budget, and operates independently from the investigated agencies.

This provides five critical protections. Physical separation means IGs aren't in agency buildings where daily pressure exists. Budget independence means agencies cannot threaten IG funding. Shared resources allow IGs to collaborate and share expertise. Cross-agency coordination allows tracking problems across multiple agencies. Protection from retaliation becomes built into the structure—agency heads cannot fire, demote, or punish IGs who work for a different organization.

Any bribe attempt must be immediately reported to the Constitutional Guardian, FBI, and included in the next IG report with full documentation. The IG may not accept, solicit, or retain any bribe or thing of value. Attempted bribery of an IG constitutes obstruction and triggers immediate investigation of the person or entity attempting the bribe.

The Constitutional Guardian coordinates IG resources and tracks patterns across all IG reports but doesn't control individual investigations. IGs remain independent investigators. The Guardian provides support and looks for problems that appear across multiple agencies while each IG maintains investigative independence.

The real power comes through the Quad Reporting Structure (reporting to four different authorities at the same time). Every IG report goes to four recipients: the Agency Head being investigated, who must respond within thirty days; the President, who can order correction or remove agency heads based on findings; Congress, which can hold hearings and investigate further; and the Constitutional Guardian, who tracks patterns and issues an annual report combining findings from across government.

This creates accountability impossible to evade. Agency heads cannot hide findings from the President. The President cannot hide findings from Congress. Congress cannot hide findings from the public because the Guardian's annual report is completely public. No single point of suppression exists.

If an agency head ignores serious problems, the President can act. If the President ignores findings, Congress can investigate. If Congress ignores violations, citizens see the Guardian's annual report and can demand action through elections.

The quad reporting also creates accountability for IGs themselves. IGs operate independently but remain accountable for accurate and honest reports. Anyone believing an IG report contains false information can challenge it through a process that protects against both IG corruption and false accusations. This ensures IGs cannot file malicious or inaccurate reports without consequences.

Complete Inspector General procedures are detailed in Appendix H.

HOW IT OVERSEES THE FBO

Chapter Seven detailed four layers preventing FBO tyranny: complete transparency with all decisions published immediately, an Inspector General embedded in FBO operations, direct Congressional oversight through Banking Committees, and external Constitutional review.

The Office of Constitutional Compliance provides two of these layers.

Division One examines FBO actions for Constitutional alignment through regular audits. Is the FBO operating within its delegated authority to enforce fiscal discipline and sound banking principles? Are spending denials based on legitimate Constitutional limits or political bias? Does the FBO respect the balance between federal and state authority and individual rights in its enforcement? These audits ensure the FBO remains servant of Constitutional principles rather than becoming an independent power.

The Constitutional Guardian receives all IG reports on FBO operations through the quad reporting structure. If the FBO IG discovers problems---bias in enforcement, exceeding authority, lack of transparency---the Guardian sees these findings simultaneously with the President and Congress. The Guardian tracks patterns in FBO operations and includes FBO assessment in the annual Constitutional compliance report.

Combined with the FBO's own Inspector General and complete public transparency, these oversight layers make FBO tyranny nearly impossible. No single point of failure exists, violations cannot be hidden, and the FBO cannot operate beyond Constitutional limits without immediate exposure and political consequences.

STATISTICS AND MEASUREMENT

The Office tracks clear, measurable statistics showing progress toward Constitutional compliance. Success is defined precisely and tracked publicly.

The primary statistic measures what percentage of federal government operates within Constitutional authority. The goal is one hundred percent—every agency and program either has Constitutional support or gets eliminated or transferred to states.

The second statistic measures whether Constitutional agencies stay within their limits. Agencies must meet six requirements: operate within Constitutional powers, respect the balance between federal and state authority, protect individual rights, maintain transparency, follow laws passed by Congress without creating new rules, and ensure accountability. The goal is one hundred percent—all Constitutional agencies operating properly.

These two statistics measure complete Constitutional compliance. The first ensures only legitimate agencies exist. The second ensures legitimate agencies operate within limits. When both reach one hundred percent, federal government operates as the Founders designed.

All statistics are published monthly and available online to every citizen. The Office operates with the same transparency it demands from agencies it oversees.

Complete statistical procedures are detailed in Appendix I.

TRANSITION AND IMPLEMENTATION

Congress can create the Office of Constitutional Compliance through normal legislative process. The Constitutional Compliance Office Establishment Act requires simple majority passage in both houses and Presidential signature—the same process used for any legislation. No Constitutional Amendment is needed. Congress has clear authority under Article I to create offices ensuring Constitutional compliance.

Complete implementation procedures are detailed in Appendix J.

RESOURCE REQUIREMENTS AND REDUCTION

The Office of Constitutional Compliance operates with a budget and staffing structure designed to shrink as it succeeds. This distinguishes it from typical government agencies that fight to preserve and expand budgets regardless of mission accomplishment.

The office operates in two distinct phases. Years One through Five require substantial resources for the Constitutional Authority Inventory---cataloging every federal agency and program, examining each against enumerated powers, and publishing findings. This heavy lift demands peak staffing of Constitutional scholars, researchers, and analysts to complete work that has never been done in American history.

Year Six forward shifts to ongoing compliance monitoring with dramatically reduced resource needs. Once unconstitutional agencies are eliminated and only Constitutional entities remain, the work becomes lighter but permanent---compliance monitoring, prevention, and IG coordination requiring far fewer staff and budget.

The budget structure could include automatic reductions tied to Primary Statistic One. As the percentage of government operating within Constitutional authority increases, budget authorization could decrease proportionally. As the inventory nears completion, the office operates with significantly reduced costs. Success is measured by approaching minimum viable operation, not by bureaucratic expansion.

Congress authorizes the Office budget annually with performance requirements. If progress stalls, Congress can reduce funding or demand changes. The office must show measurable improvement in Constitutional compliance.

This creates government designed to serve Constitutional principles rather than preserve bureaucratic empires. The Office succeeds by accomplishing its mission efficiently and then shrinking to minimal ongoing operations.

Complete budget and staffing procedures are detailed in Appendix K.

THE IDEAL SCENE

Imagine government operating exactly as the Founders designed. Federal agencies exist only where the Constitution provides clear authority, while functions beyond federal authority operate under state and local jurisdiction or through private enterprise. These state and local operations serve people directly and respond to local preferences. Citizens access all government operations and compliance information immediately through complete transparency. Agencies remain within Constitutional bounds because principles are clear, education is effective, and violations carry immediate political consequences.

This new Office of Constitutional Compliance operates with complete independence, free from political pressure or agency influence. No administration can suppress findings, no party can control the Guardian position, and Constitutional principles are applied consistently regardless of which party controls government.

Citizens trust their government because Constitutional compliance is verified continuously, violations are exposed immediately, and corrections happen publicly with clear accountability.

Federal employees work in agencies with clear Constitutional authority, understanding exactly what Constitutional powers authorize and what limits apply. Former federal workers from eliminated unconstitutional agencies contribute productively in state governments, local communities, and private enterprise. National productivity increases as people work in productive sectors rather than expanding bureaucracy without Constitutional foundation.

Government serves the people within Constitutional limits rather than ruling beyond them, the Founders' design operates as intended, and the American experiment in limited government and individual liberty functions according to its original principles.

CONCLUSION

The Office of Constitutional Compliance accomplishes what has never existed in American history: systematic proactive enforcement of Constitutional principles before violations occur, combined with comprehensive examination of whether agencies have Constitutional authority to exist at all.

For the first time, someone asks before government acts whether the Founders would have authorized this action, every agency must prove Constitutional authority supports its existence, and Constitutional compliance becomes monitored continuously rather than punished occasionally while violations become politically expensive through immediate public reporting rather than hidden through complexity.

The Office produces a clear Valuable Final Product: Government operating within Constitutional authority.

Together with the Federal Banking Office, the Office of Constitutional Compliance creates government structure where the past century's mistakes become impossible to repeat. Power is matched by accountability, authority is balanced by transparency, and structure prevents corruption rather than merely punishing it.

But what if federal reorganization is blocked, Congress refuses despite economic collapse approaching, or federal government proves incapable of reforming itself despite clear need and Constitutional authority?

Chapter Nine provides the answer: state sovereignty under the Tenth Amendment enables states to implement sound banking independently, providing both pressure on federal reform and protection if federal reform fails. States need not wait for federal action. Constitutional authority exists for states to act.

The window is narrow. The need is urgent. The path is clear.

Chapter Nine

STANDARD BANKING FOR STATES

Constitutional Authority to Act

> *"The powers delegated by the proposed Constitution to the federal government are few and defined. Those which are to remain in the State governments are numerous and indefinite."*
>
> —James Madison, Federalist 45

The Federal Banking Office represents the best federal solution. Chapters 7 and 8 showed how reformed federal banking would work. But implementing it will require tremendous effort. Those who profit from the Federal Reserve System will fight to keep their power over the American people. They won't surrender it willingly. It will have to be taken from them.

But banks and states don't need to wait for Washington to act.

Right now, today, any bank can begin implementing Standard Banking principles—no legislation required, no permission needed, no new charters—just sound banking practiced within current law.

The Federal Reserve requires zero percent reserves. That's a minimum, not a maximum. Banks can hold more. Much more. And they can hold those reserves in real assets rather than paper promises.

This chapter explains what banks can do immediately and why this action protects everyone---banks, depositors, communities, and the nation---if the Federal Reserve continues its current path to collapse.

The Standard Banking Foundations

Standard Banking rests on principles proven over centuries. Before diving into immediate implementation, understanding these principles is essential.

The Goal: Turn savings into production, increasing prosperity and survival of individuals, communities, and the nation.

Everything flows from this goal. Banking exists to serve productive businesses, not to extract wealth through financial manipulation. The banker's role is directing saved capital toward productive use that creates real value. When banking serves this goal, prosperity follows. When banking abandons this goal for speculation and debt schemes, collapse follows.

There are seven fundamental purposes that support this goal by ensuring banking serves everyone it touches—from bankers to depositors to communities (see Chapter 2).

Nine Fundamental Policies implement these purposes (detailed in Chapter 2).

These aren't new principles. They're how banking worked before the Federal Reserve corrupted it. And banks can return to these principles today.

What Banks Can do Today

The Federal Reserve mandates zero percent reserves—banks can lend every dollar deposited, holding nothing back. This is insane, but it's the rule. However, zero is the minimum, not the maximum, and banks can hold far more. A bank can announce tomorrow: "We're building to thirty-three percent reserves in silver and gold to protect our depositors." No permission is required, no regulatory approval is needed—it's the bank's choice to be more conservative than required.

Standard Banking recommends holding reserves in a combination of silver and gold.

Banks can also accept deposits directly in United States silver and gold coins. Depositors holding precious metals can open storage accounts maintaining 100% reserves with immediate access, or investment accounts operating at 33% reserves while earning interest. These precious metal accounts use silver coin face value as the unit of account, protecting depositors from dollar inflation while their wealth finances productive enterprise.

Building trust with precious metals holders requires education and proof. Skepticism is justified after a century of corrupt banking. Banks should provide every prospective depositor with materials explaining Standard Banking principles—how the accounts work, what reserves mean, why transparency matters. A copy of this book or a state-approved policy booklet gives depositors the understanding needed to trust banks again. State deposits prove the model works. Transparency and education explain why it works. Together, they rebuild trust.

United States silver coins—American Silver Eagles, pre-1965 dimes, quarters, and half-dollars, modern commemorative silver dollars—are all official United States currency, legal tender for all debts public and private. Banks can hold reserves in these silver coins instead of paper dollars. Completely legal. It's still United States money, just sound money instead of inflating paper.

If the Federal Reserve continues its current path and the dollar collapses, banks with silver reserves have a far better chance of maintaining operations and protecting depositors. They can pay in coins with real value. Banks with zero reserves or paper reserves face immediate failure—they have nothing of value to pay depositors. The FDIC can't bail out the entire banking system simultaneously. More importantly, depositors trust banks holding real reserves. That trust enables faster recovery and rebuilding when crisis passes. Sound reserves don't guarantee survival, but they provide the foundation both banks and depositors need to weather collapse and recover.

Standard Banking goes beyond reserves to focus on productive lending: financing farmers planting crops, manufacturers buying equipment, businesses creating inventory. These primary stage loans create the real commodities that back the credit extended.

Transparency will build trust. Banks should publish monthly reports showing how they're achieving banking's goal: which farms expanded production, which manufacturers bought equipment, which businesses created jobs. When depositors see their money turning into real prosperity, they understand their wealth is financing the community's growth while staying protected by real reserves.

How Silver-Based Lending Works

Standard Banking offers precious metal accounts denominated in silver coin face value, independent of dollar market prices. These accounts operate alongside traditional dollar accounts, protecting depositors from dollar inflation.

In other words, when a depositor places $100 face value in silver coins into an investment account, the bank records $100 face value—not the market value of the silver content. The depositor will receive $100 face value back plus interest, regardless of what those coins trade for in the secondary market.

For loans, the bank lends using this same silver coin face value. A farmer needing capital for spring planting borrows $93 face value in pre-1965 silver coins. The farmer uses these coins to purchase seeds, equipment, and supplies from sellers who accept silver at face value, often at substantial discounts compared to Federal Reserve Notes.

Here's how this works in practice: A seed seller might price his product at $100 in Federal Reserve Notes or $7 in silver coin face value. Why would he offer this discount? Because he receives real silver that holds value, protects him from dollar inflation, and can be used for his own purchases from other businesses accepting silver. The discount attracts customers holding silver while giving the seller sound money.

The farmer plants his crop, harvests in fall, and sells the wheat at current market prices in Federal Reserve Notes. He immediately converts these paper dollars to silver coins at the prevailing rate and repays his loan in silver face value—$93 plus $4 interest, totaling $97 face value.

The bank receives the $97 face value in silver coins. This repayment goes back into reserves, available for withdrawal by depositors or for new loans. Investment account holders receive their share of the interest earned. The silver's value increased through interest earned while the Federal Reserve Note may have depreciated through inflation. This is why accounts must be denominated in silver face value, not paper dollar amounts.

All of this can happen today within current law. Simply put: commit to Standard Banking now.

Work with your state to implement these policies and gain recognition as a Standard Bank.

BUILDING A SILVER-BASED ECONOMY

What we're describing isn't simply a banking reform. It's the foundation for a complete economic transformation where silver becomes the primary measure of value and Federal Reserve Notes become secondary.

In this economy, silver face value represents the stable measure. Prices are fundamentally set in silver coin face value, with Federal Reserve Note prices fluctuating based on the paper dollar's current purchasing power against silver. As more businesses accept silver at face value and more banks lend in silver, a parallel economy emerges—one operating on sound money principles while the Federal Reserve system continues its inflationary path.

The economic effect reverses everything the Federal Reserve created. Under Fed policy, dollars lose value over time, forcing savers into risky investments just to preserve wealth and rewarding debtors who repay loans with depreciated currency. Under Standard Banking with silver-based commerce, the opposite occurs. As productive capacity increases through sound lending to farmers and manufacturers, the supply of real goods expands. More goods competing for the same amount of silver means prices fall—not because silver lost value, but because production increased prosperity.

As the silver-based economy grows, new coins can be minted with actual precious metal content. New silver dimes, quarters, and half-dollars will contain 90% silver, just as pre-1965 coins did, while gold coins in $5, $10, $20, and $50 denominations handle larger transactions and savings. Even copper pennies and nickels will have their original value and become relevant again. The U.S. Mint can produce new coins as commerce requires them, allowing money supply to expand naturally with production, ensuring face value stays backed by real metal. Money creation follows productive capacity, not government printing presses.

This is deflation as prosperity, not deflation as crisis. When prices fall because production expanded, everyone benefits—workers' wages buy more, savers see their stored wealth gain purchasing power without risk, and businesses profit from increased sales volume even as unit prices decline. The entire community becomes wealthier through actual production rather than monetary manipulation.

Eventually, if the federal government replaces the Federal Reserve with the Federal Banking Office, the Federal Reserve Note will be reconnected to the metal economy, backed by actual silver and gold reserves, redeemable on demand, operating under sound banking principles. A currency properly backed by reserves and issued only as production expands would reverse its century-long decline. Citizens could trust their currency again. But this requires federal reform detailed in Chapters 7 and 8.

States and banks have the authority to act now. By implementing Standard Banking and building silver-based commerce networks, they create the working alternative that proves the concept, protects their communities, and generates political pressure for federal adoption. Each business accepting silver at face value, each farmer borrowing in silver, each depositor storing wealth in silver coins rather than paper dollars—these individual actions compound into economic transformation.

The contrast could not be clearer. The Federal Reserve economy runs on debt and inflation. The Standard Banking economy runs on production and sound money. Under the Fed, your wealth slowly erodes through inflation, your community finances consumption instead of production, and prosperity remains forever out of reach. Under Standard Banking, your wealth holds value, your community builds productive capacity, and prosperity compounds through actual creation. One path extracts, the other creates.

THE STATE INCENTIVE

Individual banks can implement Standard Banking on their own. But states can dramatically accelerate this transformation through smart use of state reserves.

Most states hold substantial reserves---billions in rainy day funds, pension assets, operating capital. These reserves typically sit in Treasury bonds or money market accounts, earning minimal interest while exposed to dollar devaluation.

States can do something smarter: convert reserves to United States silver coins and deposit them in your state's banks that are adopting Standard Banking principles.

The incentive is enormous. Banks want state deposits, and states make it simple: "Practice Standard Banking and you get our business." Suddenly, market pressure to adopt Standard Banking intensifies. Banks that refuse lose state deposits to competitors who comply. Customers notice which banks the state trusts with its money. Deposits flow into Standard Banking institutions.

The state's reserves are protected and invested back into their state. If the dollar collapses, state wealth is held in silver, not worthless paper. State government continues functioning because its reserves held value.

This can happen in any state today without federal permission.

For example, Florida holds $15.7 billion in budgetary reserves. In 2026, lawmakers proposed a Bitcoin reserve—digital speculation, not sound money. Better strategy: convert existing reserves to silver and gold.

The governor could announce: "Florida is converting $5 billion to United States silver and gold coins for deposit in Florida banks meeting Standard Banking criteria."

This protects wealth with real money—physical assets with intrinsic value—not digital tokens dependent on market sentiment. Silver and gold have maintained value for thousands of years. Bitcoin fluctuates wildly and becomes worthless if power fails or exchanges close.

As twenty Florida banks receive state deposits, they scale up productive lending and publish transparency reports demonstrating results. Customers notice which banks the state trusts with billions in reserves and begin moving their own deposits to these sound institutions. Competing banks, watching deposits flow to Standard Banking institutions, adopt the principles themselves to remain competitive.

Within two years, Florida has a functioning Standard Banking sector protecting businesses and communities when collapse comes.

States can maximize benefits by splitting their reserves between two account types. Keep ten to twenty percent in pure storage accounts for emergencies—these reserves remain immediately available but require storage fees. Place the remaining eighty to ninety percent into investment accounts earning interest.

Florida, placing five billion dollars strategically, might keep one billion in emergency reserves and four billion in investment accounts. That four billion earns interest while financing 2.68 billion in productive loans to Florida businesses. The state gets paid to strengthen its own economy.

THE SUPPLY CHALLENGE

Implementing Standard Banking across multiple states faces a practical problem: not enough pre-1965 silver coins exist to support widespread adoption. The solution requires states to act immediately with available resources while simultaneously pressuring Congress to authorize new coin production.

States can start today by acquiring three types of precious metal reserves. Gold bullion provides the permanent 33% reserve base that backs all lending. Silver bullion enables states to issue certificates that circulate as a medium of exchange when coins prove insufficient. Pre-1965 silver coins form the working capital that banks actually lend to farmers and manufacturers.

This combination lets states implement Standard Banking immediately while building political momentum. As more states adopt the system and demonstrate results, they collectively demand that Congress authorize the U.S. Mint to produce new 90% silver coins. States offer to provide the silver themselves—buying bullion on the open market, delivering it to the U.S. Mint for coining, and receiving the same silver back as legal tender coins after paying production costs.

When Congress authorizes new minting, everything changes. People see real money being produced again. Pre-1965-coin hoarders release their holdings because new coins eliminate scarcity. Supply expands dramatically through both new production and released hoarded coins.

States invest in precious metal reserves not for financial gain but for economic transformation. Reserves enable productive lending that expands the state economy, creates jobs, and increases tax revenue—returns that far exceed the cost of the metals themselves.

States don't wait for federal action. They implement today with available resources, prove the concept works, then demand the tools to scale it nationwide.

ALIGNMENT WITH FEDERAL REFORM

When the federal government creates the Federal Banking Office as detailed in Chapters 7 and 8, banks already operating under Standard Banking principles face seamless transition. The FBO will require exactly what these banks are already doing—thirty-three percent reserves, primary stage lending focus, transparency, and personal liability—so banks already operating this way need only continue.

Banks waiting for federal reform before acting will face painful transition. Building reserves to thirty-three percent from zero requires massive capital, and shifting loan portfolios from consumer to productive lending takes years. These banks will struggle to meet FBO requirements quickly, while banks implementing Standard Banking now gain competitive advantage both during the transition and after federal reform.

If federal reform doesn't happen—if the dollar collapses before Washington acts—banks already operating under Standard Banking have a far better chance of maintaining operations and protecting depositors. Sound reserves don't guarantee survival, but they provide the foundation both banks and depositors need to weather collapse and recover. Banks without reserves face immediate failure.

Either way, acting now provides protection and advantage.

A CALL TO ACTION

This chapter is both explanation and call to action. Banks and states possess authority to act today—to implement Standard Banking principles, to protect reserves through precious metals, to finance productive enterprises without permission or federal approval.

The Federal government was born out of the power of the States. Banking was born out of the states before there was a federal government. Banking has been corrupted at the Federal Level and wields a heavy hand to maintain its corrupt power over the banking system of America. But it only exists because you give it power to exist. Stop giving the Federal Reserve your power. Join with other bankers and your governor and working together as a team, you can return dignity and trust to banking and salvage a country that is on its way out because of perpetual government debt.

This chapter provides the vision. Appendix L provides complete implementation procedures. Your next step: share this book with someone you trust—another banker, your governor, a state legislator, a business leader. The movement starts when you start it.

This is your authority. This is your opportunity. This is your choice. What's the alternative?

Chapter Ten

THE CITIZEN'S ROLE

Standard Banking is not being offered as a favor. It is simply what should have been done in the first place—and by now, you should be able to see that.

Like the Constitution itself, Standard Banking only works when citizens choose to use it and enforce it. What follows explains how you, the American citizen—not institutions—can help bring Standard Banking into existence.

Most Americans have never heard the term Standard Banking. That is not because it is complicated, but because the system we live under has no incentive to promote an alternative to itself.

As you saw in the previous chapter, getting gold and silver into our banks is a priority as Standard Banking is implemented. While writing that chapter, I looked to see whether sufficient gold and silver coins currently exist for states to implement Standard Banking immediately. As you saw in Chapter Nine, the answer was no. The federal government would need to resume issuing them.

But that did not fully resolve the problem. We still do not know whether the federal government can be trusted to do its part. That question led me to think more deeply about where the nation's reserves actually are.

Around five o'clock one morning, lying in bed, I asked myself a simple question: What would I do with my own coins? The answer came quickly—I was already holding part of the reserves our banks would need. And then it dawned on me: Americans may collectively hold one of the largest gold and silver reserves in the nation.

Inadvertently, Americans have taken on the role of holding the nation's wealth. And just as in the days of the goldsmiths, that wealth could be deposited back into a banking system—if we knew we could trust it.

That trust can exist only if Standard Banking is implemented with full transparency.

With trust, citizens could deposit their gold and silver in local banks, receive receipts, and retain ownership of those reserves—much like in the goldsmith era. We already hold something of real value. The question is how to use that leverage to push states and banks to implement Standard Banking.

Americans can call their representatives at the local, state, and federal levels. They can speak with mayors and governors. They can offer to deposit their reserves in banks that implement Standard Banking. And they can demand that state and local governments do their part, as outlined in Chapter Nine, by placing their reserves in the form of gold and silver into local and state banks to help build the required thirty-three percent reserves.

You can demand this system—and you should. You, your community, your state, and the nation will all benefit from it. And because you already hold part of the nation's reserves, you have leverage. You can demand that officials do their jobs and provide Standard Banking.

This is the part citizens must play to make this work.

Because even if you personally hold reserves, your chances of survival in a full economic collapse are still not favorable. You cannot eat gold or silver. You can trade it for food—but if food is scarce or unavailable locally, you are still at risk.

When you invest in Standard Banking, food production and other essential needs are supported. The economy grows stronger, more resilient, and more local.

This is what we will build once we put out the fire!

Chapter Eleven

THE INVESTOR'S NEXT BIG MOVE

Capital markets are powerful tools. They can finance production, expand opportunity, and build societal and individual wealth and prosperity.

Or they can drain production and prosperity from a society, amplifying instability and leaching the life energy from the very systems that support it.

The difference is not the market itself, but the mentality that governs how capital is deployed.

The stock market does not think. It does not choose. It has no intent. It is a mechanism—one that reflects the behavior, incentives, and decisions of those who use it.

When investors direct capital toward long-term production, markets support growth. When investors direct it toward short-term extraction, markets become cannibalistic.

This creates two very different pictures of capitalism.

The first is what makes capitalism the powerful tool that builds a society. It is the high-voltage charge of currency plugged into production which greatly increases the volume of work, products, and wealth of a society.

The other picture is the dark side of personal greed, the heartless "it's just business" justification that thinks it can only win when others lose. It is the short-term gain of extracting from and reducing the currency flow of productive activities, reducing output, value, and prosperity of one's community, state, or nation.

This has been called destructive capitalism. We'll call it what it is: Capital Cannibalism.

This distorted purpose of capitalism does not require greed from everyone. It can also be encouraged through incentives that reward extraction more than creation. When the system rewards short-term gains over long-term value, behavior adapts accordingly.

The tragedy is not only that investors act within this system, but that the system trains them to believe there is no alternative to investment wealth building.

There is.

The American system never required a choice between growth and freedom. Hamilton argued for credit to finance production and national development. Jefferson warned that without constitutional limits, that same power would be abused. As we can see through this book, both were right. If they could have taken this argument one step further and reconciled their differences, they would have solved the problem as this book does. Standard Banking, done with constitutional control by State and Federal Banking Offices, unites the two ideas.

Standard Banking restores the connection between capital and production. It creates an environment where investment once again serves enterprise, labor, and real economic growth. It does not eliminate markets. It realigns them.

Under Standard Banking, capital earns returns by financing production—farms, factories, infrastructure, and businesses that create tangible value. Profits come from growth, not volatility. Wealth is built, not extracted.

Investors are not being asked to abandon markets. You are being asked to reconsider how you use markets.

You can invest in Standard Banking now as a long-term growth investment. Getting in early has always been a strategy for greater return. Investing in Standard Banking is no different, except for one point: You will be investing in the production of an entire community, an entire state, and an entire nation. The returns from such an investment will be staggering.

You can stay in the old game if you want. But when that stock market does its final death dive to the bottom and the dollar spins down to its final resting ground, you won't be spared, and all your life's work will be in ruins. You know this is true. You've seen it happen to others with these "minor" collapses we've experienced over the past 100 years. How long do you think this is going to continue?

Capital will always flow toward opportunity. But there is no opportunity in a system that destroys the free market it depends on. That only leads to an impoverished and enslaved society. This is why communism has never worked. It always reduced the free market to a black market. And everyone goes hungry.

This chapter is not a condemnation of investors. It is an invitation.

An invitation to move beyond a system that rewards cannibalism and toward one that rewards creation. To support institutions and enterprises aligned with Standard Banking principles. To apply intelligence, skill, and ingenuity toward building wealth that endures.

How do you participate? Direct capital toward banks implementing Standard Banking principles, maintaining real reserves, financing productive enterprise, publishing transparent reports. Support businesses aligned with these principles. Invest in enterprises that build rather than extract.

It's your capital, so it's your choice.

Markets will follow *your* move.

What will it be?

EPILOGUE

You have heard the shout of FIRE!

You now see the danger we are in.

What matters now is what YOU do next.

This book is the source of water that will put out the fire. The knowledge it holds will extinguish the flames. You are the fire bucket.

The water must be distributed. This knowledge must flow throughout our society—to every man, woman, and teenager. Your sex does not matter, your race does not matter, nor does your religion or your political party.

Every decent person has a part in putting out this fire. Get this knowledge into every able-bodied American's hand. Share it with your family, friends, even strangers on the street. Get it to your local banks, local leaders, state officials, and federal representatives. If you have never met these people, now is the time! Get it to every business leader you know.

When they read this book, they become another water bucket.

Be persistent! There is a fire raging and not everyone has seen it yet. Do your part!

But beware—those who started this fire want it to keep burning.

Some will try to stop your effort to round up more help. They will say it is a false alarm, or that no fire exists. They will say the buckets are empty, or that they are filled with gasoline and will just make things worse.

The best solution is to ignore these people and continue putting out the fire. You do not stop and fight mad dogs biting the tires of the firetruck. You just keep driving and ignore them.

You know the truth. You can see the fire and, more to the point, you know how to put it out.

Fortunately, there will be more people who want this fire out than those who want it to burn. You will know your friends by their response to this call.

If you run into resistance, ask this first: "Have you read the book?" Do not argue with people who have not. Tell them to read it and then come see you. They will not be helpful if they have no water, no knowledge. They are not yet a bucket.

Heroes have been said to be those who run toward the fire. Your community, your state, and your nation need heroes now.

Will you run toward the fire with water buckets in hand?

When enough of you do, the fire gets contained. Standard Banking launches. The corrupt system becomes obsolete. You build something better.

You are not alone. Thousands are reading this. Thousands are running toward the fire.

Now you act.

This is the moment. This is the choice. This is your responsibility.

Build Standard Banking. Restore Constitutional government. Distribute this knowledge until the fire is out.

We will win by acting together.

Let's put out this fire and rebuild American prosperity and our children's future.

Chapter 7 Appendices

Associated Chapter:

THE FEDERAL BANKING OFFICE

Appendix A

Federal Banking Office Appointment and Authority Framework

Author's Notice

This appendix accompanies the main text of this book and assumes familiarity with the principles and arguments developed therein. It defines strategic requirements only. Programs, projects, procedures, and implementation details are the responsibility of Congress and appropriate constitutional authorities.

Goal

To establish a constitutionally grounded Federal Banking Office with clearly defined authority and accountability.

Purposes

To ensure lawful control of money creation and regulation.
To prevent private capture of monetary authority.
To align banking oversight with constitutional intent.
To preserve public trust through transparency and accountability.

Policies

Authority shall be derived solely from constitutional and statutory law.

The Federal Banking Office shall not operate independently of constitutional oversight. Appointments shall prioritize competence, independence, and public accountability. Authority shall be limited to enumerated powers.

Plans

A Federal Banking Office shall exist with authority defined and constrained by law.
Appointment mechanisms shall ensure independence without insulation from oversight.
Oversight structures shall prevent mission expansion or private influence.

Ideal Scene

Monetary authority operates transparently under constitutional control, free from private or political capture.

Valuable Final Product

A lawful public banking authority aligned with constitutional limits.

Appendix B

Fiscal Oversight and Financial Accountability Framework

Author's Notice

This appendix defines strategic requirements only. Implementation details are the responsibility of Congress and appropriate authorities.

Goal

To ensure fiscal oversight of banking operations remains transparent, lawful, and accountable.

Purposes

To prevent misuse of public funds.
To ensure clear tracking of monetary flows.
To reinforce public accountability.

Policies

Financial reporting shall be accurate, timely, and verifiable.
Oversight mechanisms shall be independent of operational control.
Fiscal authority shall remain bounded by law.

Plans

Reporting frameworks shall support meaningful oversight.
Review mechanisms shall detect and correct misuse.

Ideal Scene

Public funds are managed transparently with no hidden liabilities.

Valuable Final Product

A fiscally accountable banking oversight structure.

Appendix C

Banking Regulation and Standards Enforcement Framework

Author's Notice
This appendix defines strategy only and does not prescribe procedures.

Goal
To enforce uniform banking standards that support productive lending and financial stability.

Purposes
To ensure banks operate within lawful reserve requirements.
To discourage speculative and extractive practices.
To protect depositors and communities.

Policies
Regulation shall prioritize production over speculation.
Standards shall be applied uniformly and predictably.
Enforcement shall be corrective, not punitive.

Plans
A standards framework shall govern reserve discipline and lending practices.
Enforcement mechanisms shall support stability without overreach.

Ideal Scene

Banks finance real economic activity under clear and fair rules.

Valuable Final Product

A stable, production-oriented banking system.

Appendix D

Oversight and Constitutional Compliance Framework

Author's Notice

This appendix defines strategic oversight requirements only.

Goal

To ensure the Federal Banking Office operates within constitutional limits.

Purposes

To prevent concentration of unchecked power.
To maintain separation of powers.
To preserve public trust.

Policies

Oversight bodies shall be independent of operational control.
Compliance reviews shall be regular and transparent.
Authority shall not expand through interpretation.

Plans

Review mechanisms shall detect and correct constitutional violations.
Accountability structures shall ensure lawful operation.

Ideal Scene

Banking oversight remains effective, lawful, and restrained.

Valuable Final Product

A constitutionally compliant banking authority.

Appendix E

System Transition and Institutional Replacement Framework

Author's Notice
This appendix addresses strategy-level transition considerations only.

Goal
To guide the orderly transition from the existing banking system to Standard Banking.

Purposes
To maintain financial continuity.
To prevent economic disruption.
To replace failing institutions lawfully.

Policies
Transitions shall prioritize stability and public confidence.
Replacement shall occur without concentration of power.
Public obligations shall be honored.

Plans
Transition frameworks shall phase out incompatible institutions.
Replacement structures shall align with Standard Banking principles.

Ideal Scene

The financial system transitions smoothly without crisis or loss of trust.

Valuable Final Product

A stable transition to Standard Banking.

Chapter 8 Appendices

Associated Chapter:

THE OFFICE OF CONSTITUTIONAL COMPLIANCE

Appendix F

Appointment and Independence Framework

Author's Notice

This appendix accompanies the main text of this book and assumes familiarity with the principles and arguments developed therein. It defines strategic requirements only. Programs, projects, procedures, and implementation details are the responsibility of Congress and appropriate constitutional authorities.

Chapter Context

Chapter 8 establishes that constitutional enforcement fails when oversight bodies are either politically dependent or structurally insulated from accountability.

Goal

To ensure the Office of Constitutional Compliance is led by constitutionally grounded, independent leadership capable of enforcing constitutional limits.

Purposes

To establish legitimate constitutional authority for compliance enforcement.

To insulate constitutional oversight from political pressure.

To prevent consolidation of unchecked enforcement power.
To maintain public trust through accountability.

Policies

The Office shall not create policy.
Appointment authority derives solely from constitutional mandate.
Independence does not exempt leadership from oversight.
Authority is limited to enumerated powers.

Plans

Leadership structures prioritize constitutional competence.
Authority boundaries are explicit and non-expandable.
Oversight mechanisms ensure lawful conduct.

Ideal Scene

The Office operates independently, transparently, and within strict constitutional limits.

Valuable Final Product

A constitutionally grounded oversight authority trusted to enforce lawful limits.

Appendix G

Constitutional Review and Enforcement Framework

Author's Notice
This appendix defines strategic requirements only.

Chapter Context
Constitutional limits lose force when enforcement is selective or discretionary.

Goal
To ensure constitutional limits are reviewed and enforced consistently.

Purposes
To prevent selective enforcement.
To correct violations early.
To preserve separation of powers.

Policies
Review is rule-based and continuous.
Enforcement is corrective, not punitive.
No policy authority is assumed.

Plans
Review frameworks evaluate actions against enumerated powers.
Enforcement mechanisms restore compliance.

Ideal Scene

Constitutional limits are enforced quietly and predictably.

Valuable Final Product

A durable constitutional enforcement system.

Appendix H

Inspector General Authority and Safeguards Framework

Author's Notice

This appendix defines strategic requirements only.

Chapter Context

Oversight bodies themselves require oversight.

Goal

To ensure internal integrity within the Office.

Purposes

To detect abuse or deviation.
To protect lawful operations.
To reinforce accountability.

Policies

Inspector General operates independently.
Authority is investigative, not operational.
Safeguards prevent retaliation.

Plans

Internal review mechanisms detect issues early.
Findings are reported lawfully.

Ideal Scene

Integrity issues are corrected without scandal.

Valuable Final Product

A trusted internal oversight mechanism.

Appendix I

Transparency, Reporting, and Statistical Integrity Framework

Author's Notice
This appendix defines strategic requirements only.

Chapter Context
Transparency must support accountability without politicization.

Goal
To ensure disciplined transparency and reliable reporting.

Purposes
To inform oversight.
To prevent data manipulation.
To reinforce public trust.

Policies
Reporting is accurate and consistent.
Statistics are protected from influence.
Disclosure does not replace enforcement.

Plans
Reporting frameworks provide visibility.
Integrity safeguards ensure reliability.

Ideal Scene

Oversight reporting is trusted and non-performative.

Valuable Final Product

A transparent, reliable reporting system.

Appendix K

Resource Requirements and Reduction Framework

Author's Notice

This appendix defines strategic requirements only.

Chapter Context

Oversight institutions should shrink as success increases.

Goal

To align resources with mission success.

Purposes

To prevent bureaucratic permanence.
To conserve public resources.
To reinforce mission discipline.

Policies

Resources scale down with compliance improvement.
Success is measured by reduced need for oversight.

Plans

Resource frameworks adjust capacity based on outcomes.
Long-term operations remain minimal.

Ideal Scene

The Office shrinks as constitutional compliance improves.

Valuable Final Product

A mission-driven institution that contracts as it succeeds.

Chapter 9 Appendix

Associated Chapter:

STANDARD BANKING FOR STATES:

THE CONSTITUTIONAL AUTHORITY TO ACT

Appendix L

State-Level Standard Banking Adoption Framework

Author's Notice

This appendix accompanies the main text of this book and assumes familiarity with the principles and arguments developed therein. It defines strategic requirements only. Programs, projects, procedures, and implementation details are the responsibility of state legislatures and appropriate constitutional authorities.

Chapter Context

Chapter 9 establishes that states possess clear constitutional authority to act when federal monetary systems fail to protect citizens. It explains that Standard Banking principles can be adopted at the state level without waiting for federal reform.

Goal

To enable states to adopt Standard Banking principles lawfully and responsibly using existing constitutional authority.

Purposes

To protect citizens from monetary instability.
To restore monetary discipline at the state level.
To encourage productive investment and economic resilience.

To reinforce constitutional federalism through lawful state action.

Policies

State action shall remain consistent with constitutional limits.
Standard Banking adoption shall prioritize stability and continuity.
States shall not assume federal monetary authority.
Coordination among states shall remain voluntary and lawful.

Plans

State-level frameworks shall apply Standard Banking principles within constitutional authority.
Legal review mechanisms shall ensure compliance with constitutional bounds.
Transition strategies shall preserve public confidence and financial continuity.

Ideal Scene

States act confidently within their constitutional authority, providing financial stability and resilience for their citizens.

Valuable Final Product

A lawful, state-driven pathway to monetary stability that strengthens federalism and protects citizens.

Glossary

Boom-Bust Cycle

A repeating pattern where the economy grows quickly and then crashes. Easy money leads to too much borrowing and spending, which looks good at first. When the limits appear, businesses fail, jobs are lost, and the economy contracts.

Capital Cannibalism

When money is used to make money without building anything real. Profits come from trading, leverage, and price swings instead of helping farms, factories, or businesses grow. Over time, this weakens the real economy.

Capital Stewardship

Using money responsibly to build things that last. This means investing in people, tools, and businesses that create real value over time instead of chasing quick gains.

Central Banking

A system where one powerful institution controls how much money exists and how easy it is to borrow. Instead of money being limited by real savings or production, it can be created by policy decisions. This puts great power in the hands of a few people and removes natural limits that normally slow debt and money growth.

Constitutional Monetary Authority

The idea that control over money should follow clear rules and limits set by the Constitution. Money should be managed openly and be accountable to the people, not controlled by private or unaccountable groups.

Credit Expansion

When new money is created by lending more than there is real value to support it. This feels good at first but later causes higher prices, bad investments, and economic trouble.

Custodial Account

A bank account meant only for safekeeping. The bank holds your money and returns it whenever you ask. The money is not supposed to be loaned out or put at risk.

Federal Banking Office (FBO)

A proposed public office that manages the nation's money using clear rules. It ensures that money is issued only when real reserves exist and that government spending stays within real limits.

Federal Reserve

1. The system created in 1913 that controls how much money exists in the United States and how easy it is to borrow. It can create new money by decision rather than by direct backing in real assets, affecting prices, debt, and savings across the economy.

2. The real resources that back a nation's money, such as gold, silver, energy, food, and other government-held assets. Under the Federal Banking Office, money is

issued only when these reserves exist, so every dollar is backed by something real.

Financialization

When making money from financial deals becomes more important than making real goods or services. The economy focuses on trading claims instead of producing things people actually need.

Inflation

When the value of money goes down over time. As more dollars are created without more real goods to support them, each dollar becomes worth less. Prices rise not because things are better, but because the money used to buy them is weaker, quietly reducing the value of savings and wages.

Investment Account

A bank account where you allow your money to be loaned out. You accept some risk in exchange for earning interest. These accounts should fund real, productive work.

Liquidity

How easily money can be paid when needed. A bank with good liquidity can return deposits on demand because it keeps money available. A bank without liquidity has most of its money tied up in loans or investments and depends on confidence or emergency help to meet withdrawals.

Long-Term Investment

Putting money into projects that take time but create real

value, like businesses, equipment, or infrastructure. Returns come from growth, not quick price changes.

Market Volatility

When prices rise and fall quickly and unpredictably. High volatility often means markets are driven by fear, speculation, or excess money rather than real value.

Monetary Distortion

When money no longer reflects real value. Prices and risks send false signals, leading people to make decisions that hurt the economy later.

Monetary Independence

The ability to live and operate without depending on unstable or dishonest money systems. It helps people and communities withstand financial crises.

Office of Constitutional Compliance

A proposed watchdog office that ensures government agencies act only within the powers granted to them by the Constitution. Its role is to enforce constitutional limits, preventing agencies from expanding their authority beyond what the law allows.

Primary-Stage Lending

Lending money directly to people who create real goods or services, such as farmers, builders, and manufacturers. This grows the real economy.

Productive Lending

Using loans to help create new goods or services. Productive lending increases real wealth instead of just moving money around.

Real Reserves

Actual valuable assets held to back money and promises. These reserves limit how much money can exist and make sure it can be paid back honestly.

Reserves

Assets a bank keeps so it can pay customers when they ask for their money. These are not everyday spending money, but backing—such as cash held aside or valuable assets—that support the bank's promises. When reserves are too low because money has been loaned out or invested, banks must rely on confidence or bailouts to survive.

Secondary-Stage Lending

Lending used to buy things that already exist instead of creating something new. For example, a loan to buy a used car helps one person buy it, but it doesn't create a new car or job. When too much lending works this way, prices rise without increasing real production.

Sound Money

Money that holds its value over time and represents real wealth. It cannot be created endlessly and forces discipline on spending and lending.

Speculation

Trying to make money from price changes instead of from producing value. When speculation dominates, instability increases.

Standard Banking

A way of banking based on honesty and limits. Banks

keep enough real value to back the money they promise, and loans are used to build real things. The goal is stability and shared prosperity.

Value Creation

Making goods or services that improve people's lives. Value creation is the foundation of real wealth.

Wealth Extraction

Taking value from others without creating anything in return. This often happens through inflation, debt systems, or bailouts that shift losses onto the public.

ABOUT THE AUTHOR

David R. Young, a successful businessman and professional home designer. He performed as a solo singer/songwriter in his 20s on the Jersey shore. David has been interested in and has studied religious philosophy and the spiritual nature of man for the past 50 years.

While a registered Independent (now Republican) who has always voted with an eye toward the Constitution, David began studying the political spectrum in August of 2011.

After establishing the dichotomy of Freedom vs Enslavement in his Book The Political Spectrum, David observed that many other aspects of society could also be plotted on this spectrum. And so he set out to research and document these as well.

Though this book was not what he had planned for Economic systems, this particular subject was seen a a grave danger to the survival of the U.S. And so it became a priority.

David lives in Florida with his wife and son.

You can email David at **dryoung.freedom@gmail.com**. He is interested in hearing your view of the subjects he writes about.

Made in United States
Troutdale, OR
11/03/2026

56847382R00110